PENNY HES YASSOUR

TEMP-EST

EDITION CANTZ

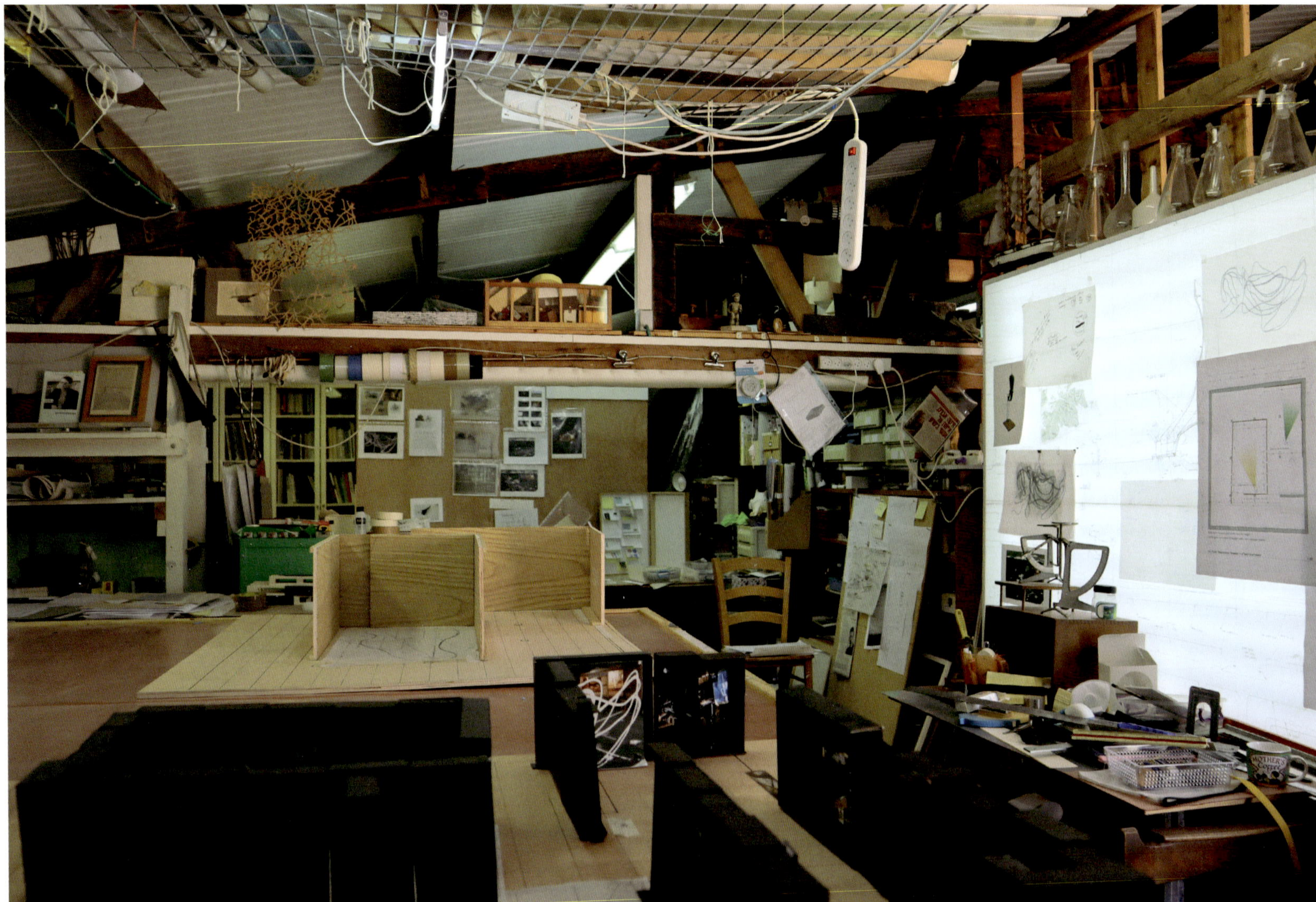

PENNY HES YASSOUR

TEMP-EST

KUNSTAUSSTELLUNG DER RUHRFESTSPIELE RECKLINGHAUSEN
KUNSTHALLE RECKLINGHAUSEN
2019

CONTENTS

INHALT

TEMP-EST

PENNY HES YASSOUR IN RECKLINGHAUSEN

HANS-JÜRGEN SCHWALM

Art exhibitions have been part of the Ruhrfestspiele cultural festival for almost seventy years. Since the 1990s, they have taken the form of solo shows dedicated on the whole to internationally active contemporary artists such as Jannis Kounellis and Per Kirkeby, Tadashi Kawamata, Ayşe Erkmen, and Magdalena Jetelová, Tatsuo Miyajima, Jan Fabre, and Daniel Buren, to name just a few. Moreover, they have all been inspired by the atmosphere of the exhibition venue where and for which they are working, looking into its history and links to society, its cultural semantics, and its everyday reality. In spite of their very different artistic approaches, their site-specific projects have all shown that local contexts are a crucial filter that enables us to understand global processes and globally distributed images and permits them to permeate our everyday lives and attain meaning.

The 2019 festival marks Olaf Kröck's debut as director of the Ruhrfestspiele Recklinghausen, which this year takes the motto "Poesie und Politik" (Poetry and Politics) as its theme. It provides an opportunity to introduce Israeli artist Penny Hes Yassour via four multimedia installations in which she combines sound, images, and a poetic realm of objects. Hes Yassour conducts an intensive exploration of the concepts of space and time, allowing us to take a fresh look at and reexperience spaces in which we live and interact with others. She transforms them with her slow-motion camerawork, which seems to keep time standing still, revealing her filmic worlds behind the visible surface and interpreting them in an explicitly political manner. Her three-dimensional images created specifically for Recklinghausen bear the descriptive titles *Space and its Double – Observations*, *Resonance Towers – between Memory and Oblivion*, *a·ban·don·ment*, and *Eroded Landscapes*.

TEMP-EST

PENNY HES YASSOUR IN RECKLINGHAUSEN

HANS-JÜRGEN SCHWALM

Die Kunstausstellungen der Ruhrfestspiele blicken mittlerweile auf eine fast siebzigjährige Geschichte zurück. Seit Anfang der 1990er-Jahre widmen sie sich monografisch vor allem international arbeitenden Künstlerinnen und Künstlern der Gegenwart wie Jannis Kounellis und Per Kirkeby, Tadashi Kawamata, Ayşe Erkmen und Magdalena Jetelová, Tatsuo Miyajima, Jan Fabre und Daniel Buren, um nur einige zu nennen. Sie alle ließen sich immer auch von der Atmosphäre des Ausstellungsorts inspirieren, für den und an dem sie arbeiteten, befragten seine Historie und gesellschaftliche Vernetzung, seine kulturelle Semantik und Lebenswirklichkeit. Trotz ihrer so unterschiedlichen künstlerischen Ansätze zeigten die jeweils *site-specific* realisierten Projekte, dass lokale Kontexte ein entscheidender Filter sind, um globale Prozesse und weltweit zirkulierende Bilder überhaupt erst begreifbar werden zu lassen, sodass sie in den Alltag dringen und Bedeutung erlangen können.

Das Festival 2019, mit dem Olaf Kröck unter dem Motto „Poesie und Politik" sein Debüt als Intendant der Ruhrfestspiele gibt, bietet Gelegenheit, die israelische Künstlerin Penny Hes Yassour mit vier multimedialen Installationen vorzustellen, in denen sie Ton, Bild und eine poetische Objektwelt zusammenbringt. Hes Yassour setzt sich intensiv mit den Themen Raum und Zeit auseinander und macht Räume, die immer auch Lebensräume, gesellschaftliche Räume sind, neu sicht- und erfahrbar. Sie verwandelt sie, indem sie mit ihrer „entschleunigten", die Zeit gleichsam anhaltenden Kameraführung hinter die bloße Oberfläche ihrer Filmwelten blicken lässt, und interpretiert sie dabei ausdrücklich auch politisch. Ihre für Recklinghausen entwickelten Raumbilder tragen die sprechenden Titel *Space and its Double – Observations, Resonance Towers – between Memory and Oblivion, a·ban·don·ment* und *Eroded Landscapes*.

Penny Hes Yassour lives and works at Kibbutz Ein Harod (Ihud) in Galilee. She has taught at the Bezalel Academy of Arts and Design in Jerusalem since 2000. In 1999 she won the Arnold Bode Award of the documenta City of Kassel, the following year she received the Award of the Adolph & Esther Gottlieb Foundation in New York, and in 2009 she was awarded the inaugural Prize for Excellence in the Arts in Israel. In recent years, she has taught classes at HafenCity Universität Hamburg and at Bard College Berlin, A Liberal Arts University, and in 2009 she designed the set for Shakespeare's *The Tempest* at Theater Freiburg.

Penny Hes Yassour tells stories and keeps history alive; she finds images for the past and the future. At documenta X, for example, she explored the role played by the German railway company Deutsche Reichsbahn in conducting the Nazis' wars of aggression and vividly conveyed the importance of its logistic operations as part of the Holocaust's machinery of extermination.

One of the four installations produced in Recklinghausen, *Resonance Towers – between Memory and Oblivion*, takes the observer through the "no man's land" of the southern Jordan Valley, which almost in its entirety (with the exception of the section between the Sea of Galilee and Beit Sche'an) forms the border between Israel and Jordan. A seemingly harmless natural idyll is revealed that is, however, permeated by barbed wire fences, rhythmically punctuated by tightly packed abandoned watchtowers, all robbing the landscape of its supposed innocence. A morbid assemblage, marked by decay and destruction, of furniture and the wreckage of architectural models throws a dark shadow on the scenery. The camera glides sedately through the Jordan Valley, stretching out time as if it were on a search for clues, although admittedly not the same clues as those sought by a geographer, biologist, or military historian. Hes Yassour's view through the lens questions what is ostensibly the "green border" along the River Jordan in a manner that is highly subjective and emotional: her view correlates history and the present day—that conglomerate of fears, hopes and wishes—thereby inserting the landscape into a network of individual and political references. Yet, above all, it is a view that wrests remembrance from forgetting. Instead of following well-trodden paths or objective cartography, it allows itself to become distracted and choose its own course, ultimately enabling it to look back with confidence.

In a certain respect, Hes Yassour's duplicated video installation *Space and its Double – Observations* forms a counterpart to this piece. It uses documentary film material from the Weizmann Institute of Science in Rechovot, Israel—or more precisely, the Department of Neurobiology—which is conducting a long-term study of the flight patterns of bats in enclosed spaces. It has long been known that these nocturnal winged creatures continually change their call depending on their surroundings. In the open air, for example, their calls are longer, louder, and less frequency modulated than when they are

Penny Hes Yassour lebt und arbeitet im Kibbuz Ein Harod (Ihud) in Galiläa. Seit 2000 lehrt sie an der Bezalel Academy of Arts and Design in Jerusalem. 1999 gewann sie den Arnold-Bode-Preis der documenta-Stadt Kassel, 2000 den Preis der Adolph & Esther Gottlieb Foundation in New York und 2009 den zum ersten Mal vergebenen Prize for Excellence in the Arts in Israel. In den vergangenen Jahren hatte sie Lehraufträge an der HafenCity Universität Hamburg – Universität für Baukunst und Metropolenentwicklung sowie am Bard College Berlin, A Liberal Arts University und schuf 2009 das Bühnenbild für William Shakespeares *The Tempest (Der Sturm)* am Theater Freiburg.

Penny Hes Yassour erzählt Geschichten und hält Geschichte wach; sie findet Bilder für die Vergangenheit und für die Zukunft. Auf der documenta X etwa thematisierte sie die Rolle der Deutschen Reichsbahn bei der Durchführung der Angriffskriege des NS-Staates und führte eindringlich die Bedeutung ihrer Logistik innerhalb der Vernichtungsmaschinerie des Holocaust vor Augen.

Eine der vier in Recklinghausen realisierten Installationen, *Resonance Towers – between Memory and Oblivion,* nimmt den Betrachter mit in das „Niemandsland" des Jordantals, das in seinem beinahe gesamten südlichen Verlauf (mit Ausnahme der Strecke vom See Genezareth bis Bet Sche'an) die Grenze zwischen Israel und Jordanien bildet. Es offenbart sich eine scheinbar harmlose Naturidylle, die allerdings noch immer von Stacheldrahtzäunen durchzogen und durch eine dichte Folge alter Wachtürme rhythmisiert wird – um so der Landschaft ihre vermeintliche Unschuld zu rauben. Eine morbide, von Verfall und Zerstörung gezeichnete Assemblage aus Möbelstücken und desaströsen Architekturmodellen wirft ihren dunklen Schatten auf die Szenerie. Der langsame, Zeit dehnende Gang der Kamera durch das Jordantal gleicht einer Spurensuche, wenngleich nicht der eines Geografen, Biologen oder Militärhistorikers. Hes Yassours Blick durch das Objektiv befragt die nur vorgeblich „grüne Grenze" entlang des Jordans höchst subjektiv und emotional: Ihr Blick bezieht Historie und Gegenwart, dieses Konglomerat aus Ängsten, Hoffnungen und Wünschen, aufeinander und verspannt die Landschaft so in ein Netz aus individuellen und politischen Bezügen. Vor allem aber entreißt er die Erinnerung dem Vergessen. Er folgt keinen ausgetretenen Pfaden, keiner objektivierenden Kartografie, sondern lässt sich ablenken und schlägt eigene Wege ein, um sich am Ende selbstbewusst umzuwenden.

In gewissem Sinne ein Pendant dieser Arbeit bildet Hes Yassours gedoppelte Videoinstallation *Space and its Double – Observations*. Sie greift auf filmisches Dokumentationsmaterial des Weizmann Institute of Science im israelischen Rechovot, genauer: dessen Fachbereich für Neurobiologie, zurück, wo man in einer Langzeitstudie den Flug von Fledermäusen in geschlossenen Räumen untersucht. Seit Langem weiß man, dass die nachtaktiven Flieger ihren Ruf ständig der jeweiligen Raumsituation anpassen. In offenem Gelände etwa sind die Rufe länger, lauter und weniger frequenzmoduliert als

close to background objects or in the process of catching insects. Research therefore focuses on the question of whether bats remember spatial dimensions—and if they do, how—and how this memory is reflected in the way they fly and their social behavior, something which could be critical to their survival. Visitors experience the experiment's claustrophobic setting up close as they make their way through a cramped, labyrinthine spatial installation. The twin rooms almost mirror each other, appealing to the visitors' capacity to remember; these spaces make it clear that we are only able to find our way in the world thanks to our memory, and without it we would lose control of our lives. Our personal identity would vanish. As the US-American psychologist Daniel L. Schacter succinctly puts it: "We are memory."

The video installation *a·ban·don·ment* traces the wild airborne gyrations of a huge murmuration of birds, twisting and turning somewhere in a "limitless" sky yet without following a common rhythm and seemingly neither conditioned nor coordinated. Above the shadows of architectural fragments and a bizarre realm of objects that move simultaneously, promising to provide a steadfast durability and universal—that is, synchronized—order to the Here and Now, the chaotic flight rips this promise apart to reveal the supposedly unwavering power of stability, of permanence as a way of life or as phantasmagoria. The birds' wild flight reflects the transitory identity of the world, with identity represented as an event. *Panta rhei*, as Heraclitus once said so fittingly: everything flows and nothing remains still; there is only becoming and transformation, which is why it is not possible to step twice into the same stream.

The fourth installation, *Eroded Landscapes*, is a film in which Hes Yassour follows the brutal interventions into a hitherto pristine landscape with "poetic" finesse. As though in a bad dream, the powerful diggers bite into the ground while trucks circle around them and groups of young men cover the site with a second skin of shimmering silver plastic sheets. Gradually burying the landscape, the sheets seemingly permit no life to exist beneath them. Only memories keep its original appearance alive, denouncing its destruction. Ultimately a completely new, reshaped terrain gleams in the dazzling sunlight, disturbingly artificial like a gigantic stage. But it is also a stage where politics and economics can promote themselves, where each and every promise and crime seems possible. It is as fascinating as it is horrifying.

Penny Hes Yassour's works for the Kunsthalle Recklinghausen are theatrical narrative spaces where we, the public, are confronted both by our own sentiments and by those of society, which invariably include fears. These spaces are highly topical and yet at the same time eternally relevant.

This exhibition could not have been brought to fruition as a sole effort. Special thanks go to Penny Hes Yassour, who responded to our invitation with such great enthusiasm. I am hugely grateful to her for the resulting intense exchange of ideas and also for the trust she placed in us right from the start. It gave us a real boost in realizing an exhibition project that,

in der Nähe von Hintergründen oder beim Fang eines Insekts. Die Forschung konzentriert sich deshalb auf die Frage, ob und wenn ja, wie sich Fledermäuse an Raumdimensionen erinnern und wie sich die Erinnerung in ihrem Flug- und Sozialverhalten niederschlägt, kann sie doch für das Überleben der Tiere bedeutsam sein. Die klaustrophobische Situation des Experiments erlebt der Ausstellungsbesucher bei seinem Gang durch eine enge, labyrinthische Rauminszenierung hautnah. Die gedoppelten, nahezu spiegelbildlich eingerichteten Räume appellieren an sein Erinnerungsvermögen; sie machen klar, dass erst die Erinnerung dazu befähigt, sich in der Welt zurechtzufinden, und einem ohne Erinnerung das Leben entgleitet. Ohne sie verflüchtigt sich die persönliche Identität, oder wie es der US-amerikanische Psychologe Daniel L. Schacter knapp resümierte: „Wir sind Erinnerung."

Die Videoinstallation *a·ban·don·ment* verfolgt den wild kreisenden Flug eines riesigen Vogelschwarms, der im Irgendwo eines „grenzenlosen" Himmels durcheinanderwirbelt, keinem gemeinsamen Rhythmus folgt und weder konditioniert noch koordiniert erscheint. Über den Schatten architektonischer Fragmente und einer bizarren Objektwelt, die im Gleichtakt ihrer Bewegung dem Hier und Jetzt eine unverbrüchliche Dauer und universelle, das heißt synchronisierte Ordnung zu geben verspricht, lässt der chaotische Vogelflug dieses Versprechen zerplatzen und entlarvt die vermeintlich unerschütterliche Kraft des Immergleichen, die Dauer als Lebensmodell, als Phantasmagorie. Im wilden Flug der Vögel spiegelt sich die transitorische Identität von Welt, stellt sich Identität als Ereignis dar. „Panta rhei", wie es bereits Heraklit auf den Punkt brachte, alles fließt und nichts bleibt; es gibt nur ein Werden und Wandeln, weshalb man eben nicht zweimal in denselben Fluss steigen kann.

In der vierten Installation, *Eroded Landscapes,* verfolgt Hes Yassour mit „poetischem" Fingerspitzengefühl die brachialen Eingriffe in eine bis dahin sich selbst überlassene Landschaft. Wie in einem bösen Traum fressen sich mächtige Bagger ins Erdreich, kreisen Trucks um sie herum und ziehen Gruppen junger Männer silbrig schimmernde Plastikbahnen wie eine zweite Haut über das Gelände. Unter ihnen, da sie kein Leben zuzulassen scheinen, wird die Landschaft nach und nach begraben. Nur noch Erinnerungen halten ihr ursprüngliches Profil wach und klagen dessen Zerstörung an. Zuletzt erstrahlt in gleißendem Sonnenlicht ein völlig neues, überformtes Landschaftsbild, das in seiner verstörenden Künstlichkeit einer gigantischen Bühne gleicht, einer Bühne auch politischer und ökonomischer Selbstdarstellung, auf der jedes Versprechen und jedes Verbrechen möglich zu sein scheint – was gleichermaßen fasziniert und erschreckt.

So entwirft Penny Hes Yassour für die Kunsthalle Recklinghausen dem Theater verwandte, narrative Räume, in denen das Publikum mit eigenen wie gesellschaftlichen Stimmungen, die immer auch Ängste beinhalten, konfrontiert wird. Sie sind höchst aktuell und zugleich zeitlos gültig.

although so stunningly effective, has proved challenging in so many respects. Further thanks are owed to Nerya Shohat, whose extreme dedication and constructive accompaniment have been critical in staging this exhibition so successfully. Not only did he provide vital impetus for Penny Hes Yassour's work, he also sensitively talked through and realized the exhibition design with her.

Again, I would like to state my deep gratitude to Sparkasse Vest Recklinghausen and its chairman, Director Dr. Michael Schulte. With their generous support, they have once again affirmed the exceedingly sympathetic interest with which they have backed our work for many years. My heartfelt thanks are also due to Stiftung Sparkasse Vest Recklinghausen for its committed support of this exhibition, which similarly played a decisive role in its success.

I would like to extend my sincere thanks to Artis in New York, whose generous support of the exhibition transcended national borders; special thanks go specifically to the executive director, Hillit Zwick, and the associate director of programs, Elena Levi, both of whom were always available for constructive and attentive communication.

I am similarly indebted to Dr. Galia Bar Or and Dr. Nimrod Reitman for their insightful catalogue texts, which vividly illustrate the full complexity of Penny Hes Yassour's artistic oeuvre and take the reader on an enlightening tour around the exhibition. The cordial and competent cooperation with Dr. Doris Hansmann at Edition Cantz was crucial in determining the appearance of the catalogue and is much appreciated.

I am obliged to Alistair Overbruck in Cologne, who once again brings a sure touch to his evocative photographic documentation of the exhibition.

This is an ideal point to thank the numerous benefactors who generously supported Penny Hes Yassour and by extension the Ruhrfestspiele exhibition project. It would have been difficult to organize the exhibition without their dedication and enthusiasm. I would thus like to acknowledge the following:

Professor Yosef Gruenbaum, Alexander Silberman Institute of Life Sciences, Hebrew University of Jerusalem.

Professor Nachum Ulanovsky, Department of Neurobiology, Weizmann Institute of Science, Rechovot.

Joachim Neuroth, Joachim Neuroth GmbH, Montabaur.

Paul Trinker, Berlin, who displayed foresight in his coordination of the exhibition's media technology and invariably proved to be a reliable contact.

Professor Jonathan Berger, Department of Music, Stanford University, who created wonderfully empathetic sound collages to accompany Penny Hes Yassour's videos.

Anat Even, Tel Aviv-Jaffa, for her conceptual accompaniment to the video film *Eroded Landscapes*.

Allein wäre dieses Ausstellungsprojekt nicht zu realisieren gewesen. Besonderer Dank gilt Penny Hes Yassour, die sich auf die Einladung unseres Hauses mit großem Enthusiasmus einließ. Ich danke ihr sehr für den intensiven gedanklichen Austausch, aber auch für das Vertrauen, das sie uns von Anfang an entgegenbrachte und das uns in dem Vorhaben bestärkte, dieses in vielfacher Hinsicht fordernde, aber auch staunend machende Ausstellungsprojekt zu realisieren.

Danken möchte ich an dieser Stelle auch Nerya Shohat für seine überaus engagierte Mitarbeit und konstruktive Begleitung des Ausstellungsprojekts, ohne die es nicht so erfolgreich hätte verwirklicht werden können. Er gab nicht nur der künstlerischen Arbeit Penny Hes Yassours wichtige Impulse, sondern hat gemeinsam mit ihr auch die Ausstellungsinszenierung sensibel durchdacht und realisiert.

Wieder einmal gilt mein herzlicher Dank der Sparkasse Vest Recklinghausen und ihrem Vorstandsvorsitzenden Dr. Michael Schulte. Durch ihre großzügige Unterstützung bekundeten sie erneut die seit vielen Jahren bewährte Zusammenarbeit und überaus wohlwollende Begleitung unserer Arbeit. Herzlich danken möchte ich aber auch der Stiftung Sparkasse Vest Recklinghausen, die das Ausstellungsprojekt engagiert förderte und damit ebenfalls zu seinem Gelingen entscheidend beitrug.

Gleichermaßen sei Artis Grants, New York, an dieser Stelle sehr herzlich für die großzügige und Grenzen überschreitende Unterstützung der Ausstellung gedankt, namentlich Hillit Zwick, Executive Director, und Elena Levi, Associate Director of Programs, die jederzeit ansprechbar waren und eine immer konstruktive und zugewandte Kommunikation pflegten.

Ein ebenso herzlicher Dank gilt Dr. Galia Bar Or und Dr. Nimrod Reitman für ihre einfühlsamen Katalogtexte, die das künstlerische Tun Penny Hes Yassours in seiner Komplexität anschaulich machen und die Ausstellung so erhellend durchlaufen. Dr. Doris Hansmann, Edition Cantz, danke ich für die stets herzliche und kompetente Zusammenarbeit, die das Erscheinungsbild des Katalogs wesentlich bestimmte.

Für die fotografische Dokumentation bedanke ich mich herzlich bei Alistair Overbruck, Köln, der wieder einmal mit sicherem Gespür auf eine Ausstellung reagierte und sie in seinen Fotografien nacherleben lässt.

Den zahlreichen Förderern, die Penny Hes Yassour und damit auch das Ausstellungsprojekt der Ruhrfestspiele wohlwollend unterstützten, sei hier ebenfalls sehr herzlich gedankt. Ohne ihr Engagement und ihre Begeisterung hätte sich die Ausstellung nicht so leicht realisieren lassen. Mein Dank gilt deshalb:

Professor Dr. Yosef Gruenbaum, Alexander Silberman Institute of Life Sciences, Hebrew University of Jerusalem

Professor Dr. Nachum Ulanovsky, Department of Neurobiology, Weizmann Institute of Science, Rechovot

Joachim Neuroth, Joachim Neuroth GmbH, Montabaur

Thanks are also due to Zvi Bar Haim and Zimri Ron, RICOR Cryogenic & Vacuum Systems, Ein Harod (Ihud).
Credit is also due to Gabriele Bültmann, managing director of the training institute Bildungszentrum des Handels e.V. and her team in the paint workshop, namely Oliver Buchholz and Hubert-Hartmut Trockel, who, along with their trainees, accompanied the construction of the exhibition with sheer dedication and helped us to overcome staff shortages.
Last but not least, I would like to thank the staff of the Ruhrfestspiele and the museums of Recklinghausen for the enormous enthusiasm, foresight, and ultimately patience with which they helped master such an important project for the festival, for the region, and for us as an organization. Not for the first time, I am grateful to my colleague Kerstin Weber for the lively exchange of ideas while planning and realizing the exhibition as well as her kind solidarity in overcoming all the challenges.

Paul Trinker, Berlin, der die Medientechnik der Ausstellung mit Weitblick koordinierte und immer ein verlässlicher Ansprechpartner war

Professor Jonathan Berger, Department of Music, Stanford University, der wunderbar einfühlsame Sound-Collagen zu den Videos von Penny Hes Yassour schuf

Anat Even, Tel Aviv-Jaffa, für ihre konzeptionelle Begleitung des Videofilms *Eroded Landscapes*

sowie Zvi Bar Haim und Zimri Ron, RICOR Cryogenic & Vacuum Systems, Ein Harod (Ihud)

Herzlich danke ich Gabriele Bültmann, Geschäftsführerin des Bildungszentrums des Handels e.V., und ihrem Team der Malerwerkstatt, namentlich Oliver Buchholz und Hubert-Hartmut Trockel, die den Ausstellungsaufbau mit ihren Auszubildenden überaus engagiert begleiteten und personelle Engpässe zu überwinden halfen.

Last, but not least danke ich den Mitarbeiterinnen und Mitarbeitern der Ruhrfestspiele und der Museen der Stadt Recklinghausen, die mit großem Engagement, Umsicht und schließlich auch immenser Geduld dazu beitrugen, das für die Ruhrfestspiele, die Region und unser Haus so wichtige Projekt zu meistern. Meiner Kollegin Kerstin Weber danke ich wieder einmal für den regen Gedankenaustausch während der konzeptionellen Vorbereitung der Ausstellung und ihrer Realisation sowie für ihre freundschaftliche Solidarität bei der Bewältigung aller Widrigkeiten.

SPACE AND ITS DOUBLE – OBSERVATIONS

Bei den Videofilmen handelt es sich um gekürzte Dokumentationen wissenschaftlicher Experimente zu räumlichem und sozialem Gedächtnis sowie räumlicher und sozialer Kognition am Fachbereich für Neurobiologie des Weizmann Institute of Science in Rechovot, Israel.

The video films are abridged documentaries of scientific experiments on spatial and social memory as well as spatial and social cognition at the Department of Neurobiology of the Weizmann Institute of Science in Rechovot, Israel.

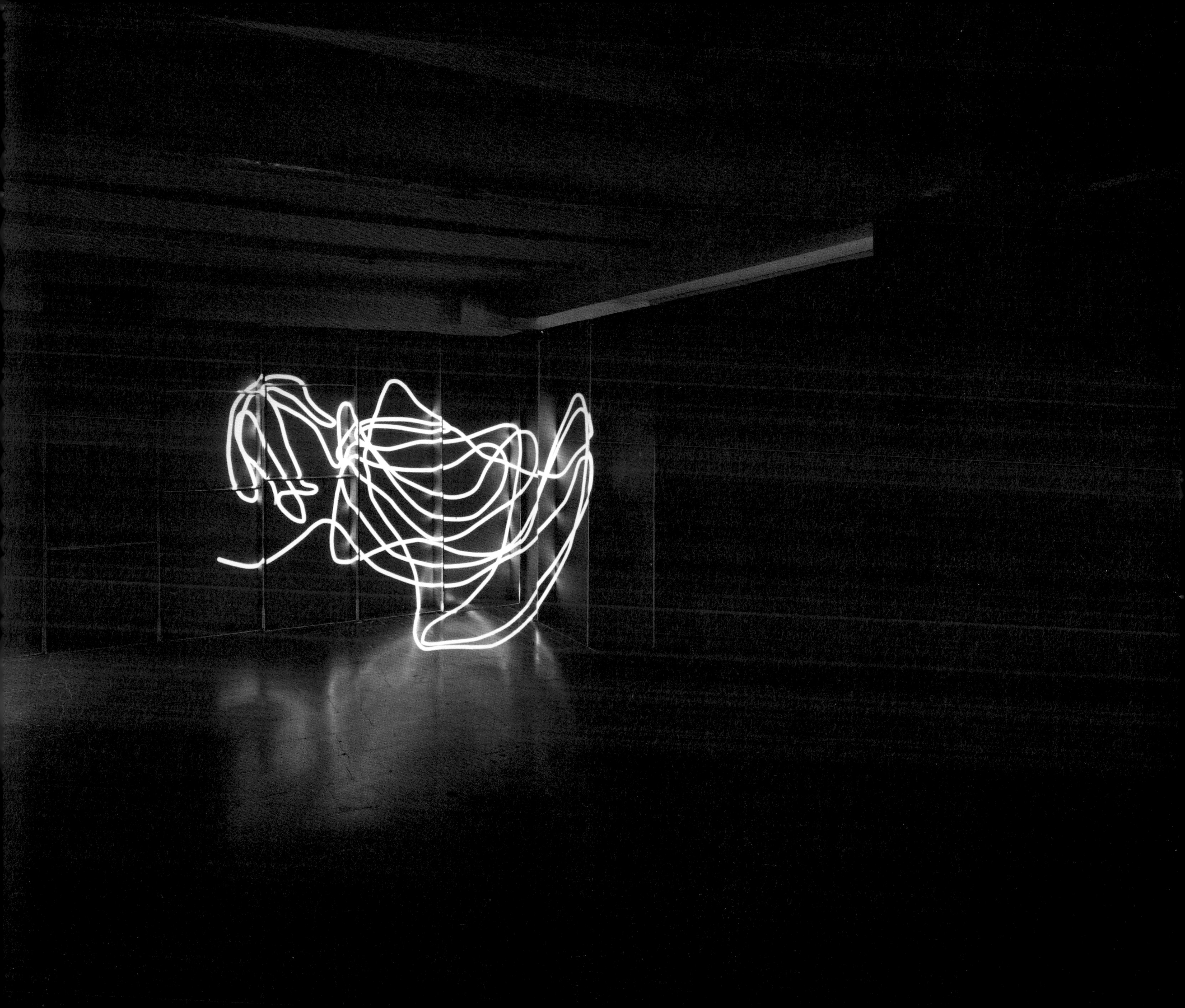

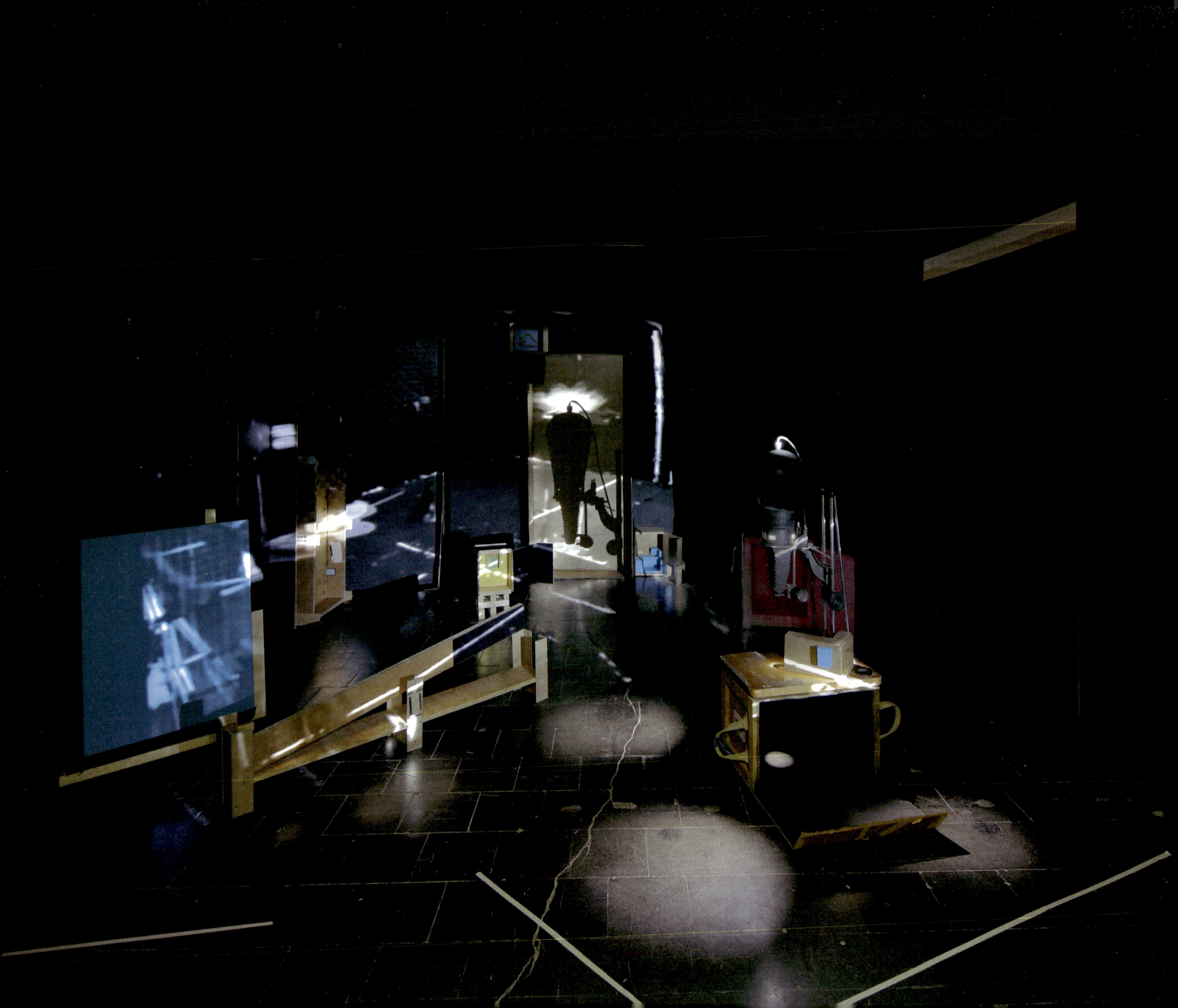

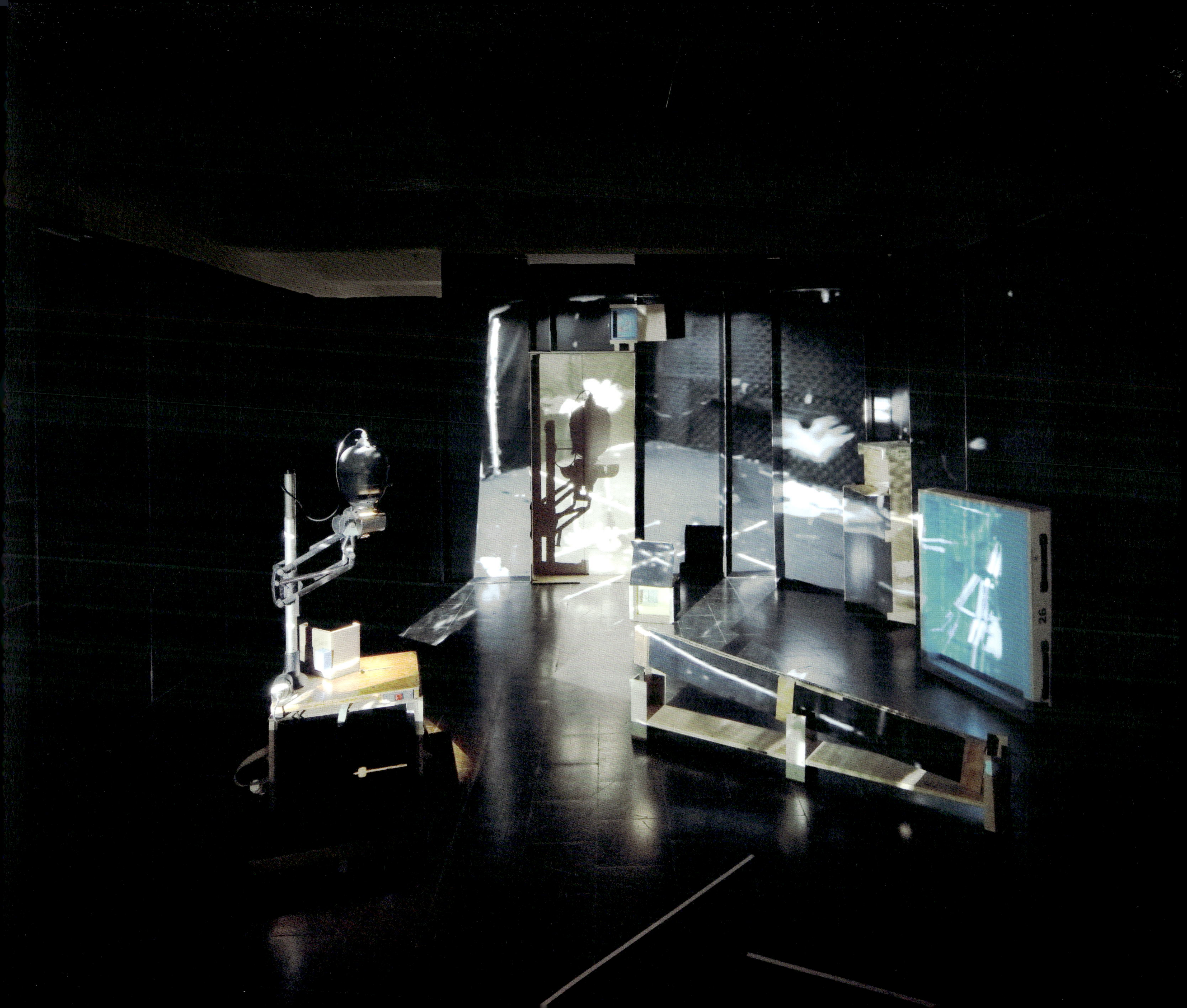
26

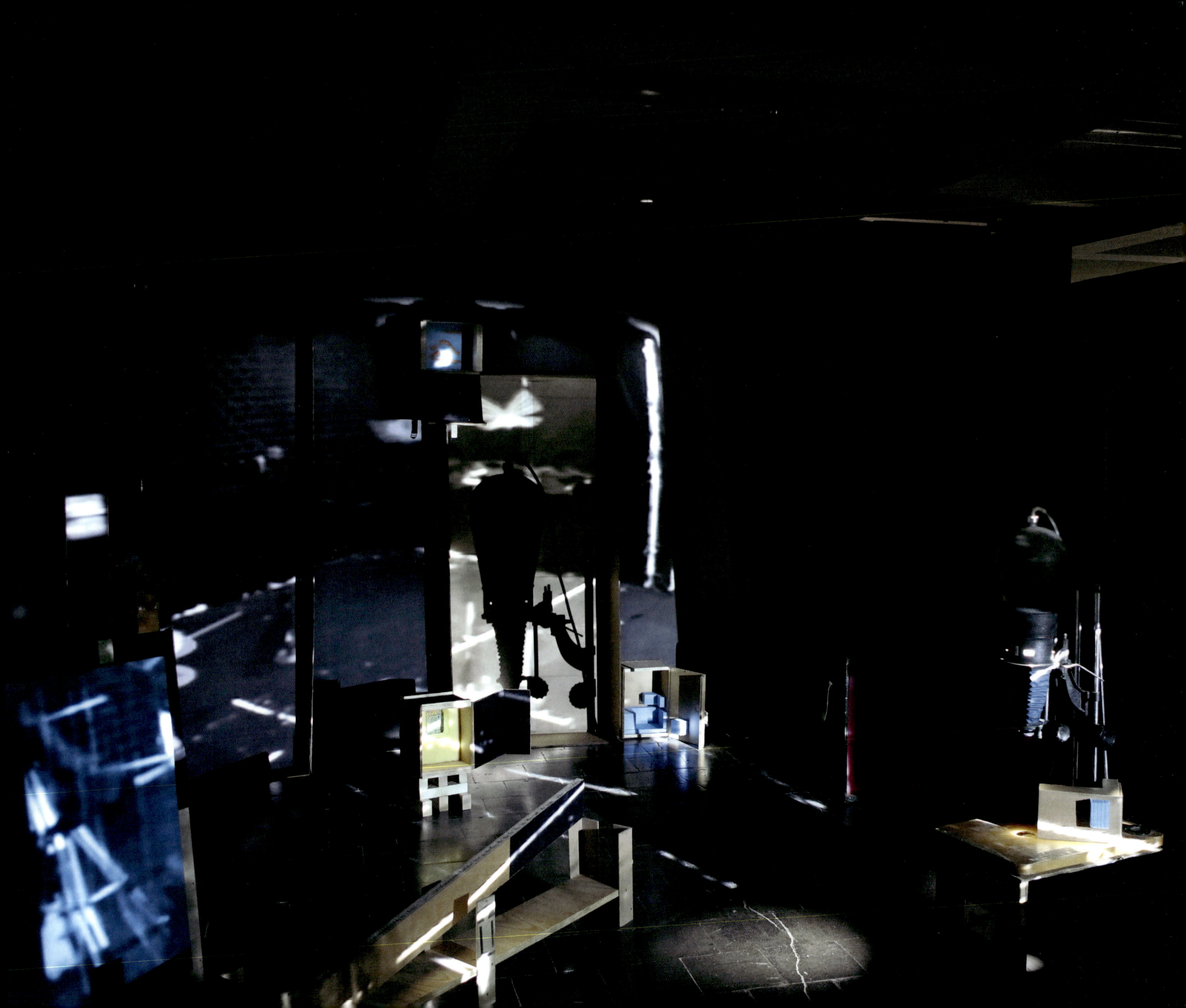

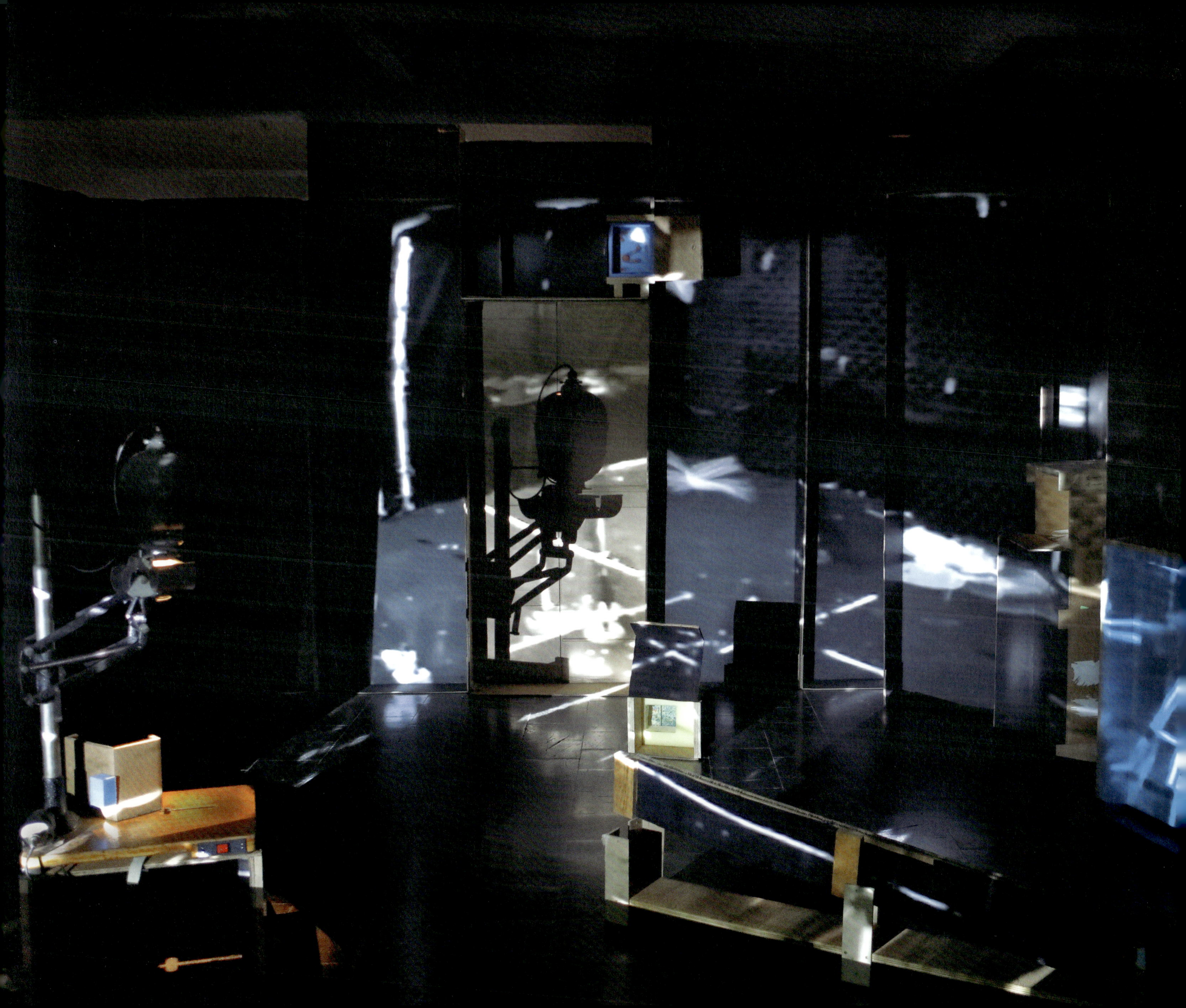

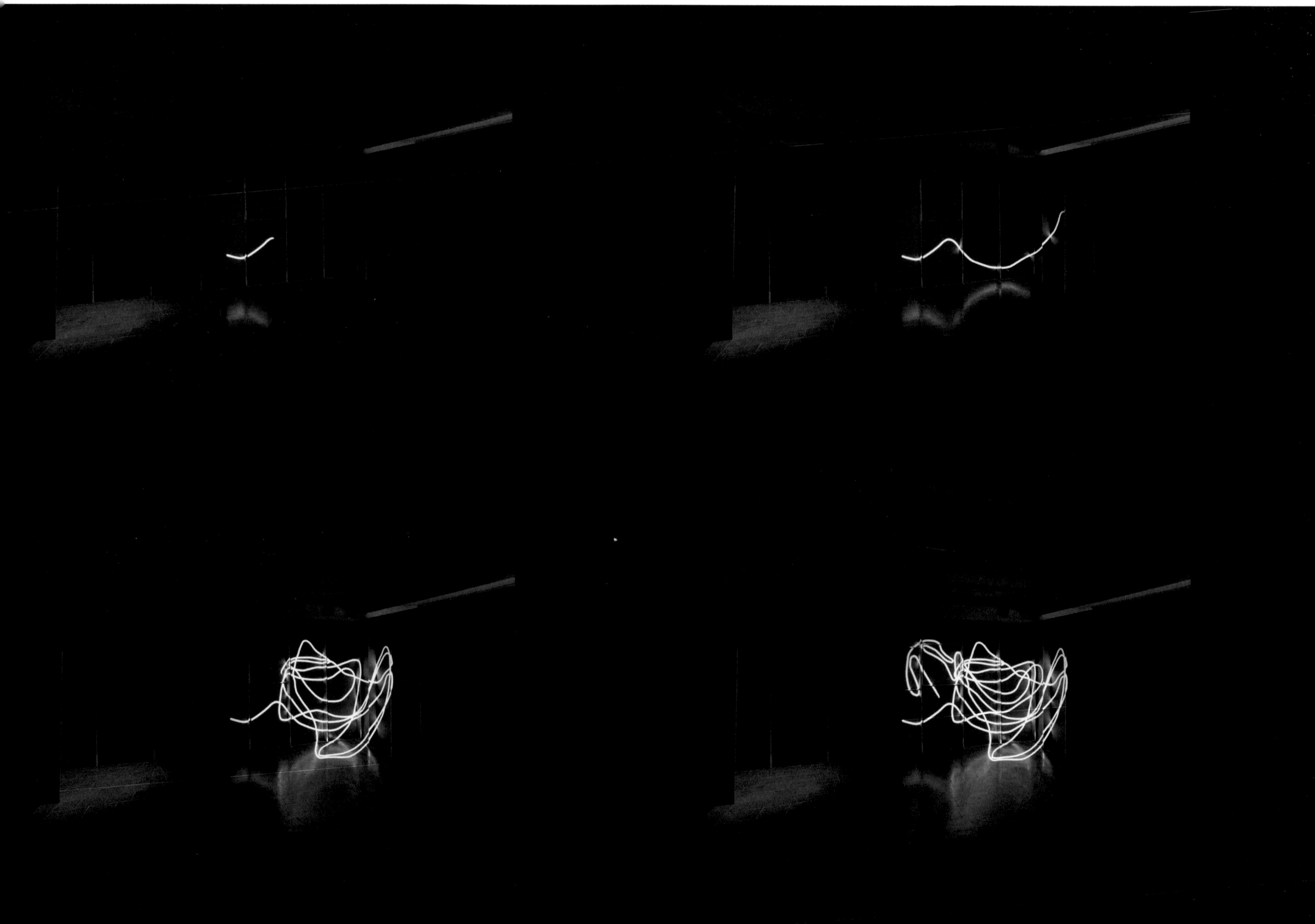

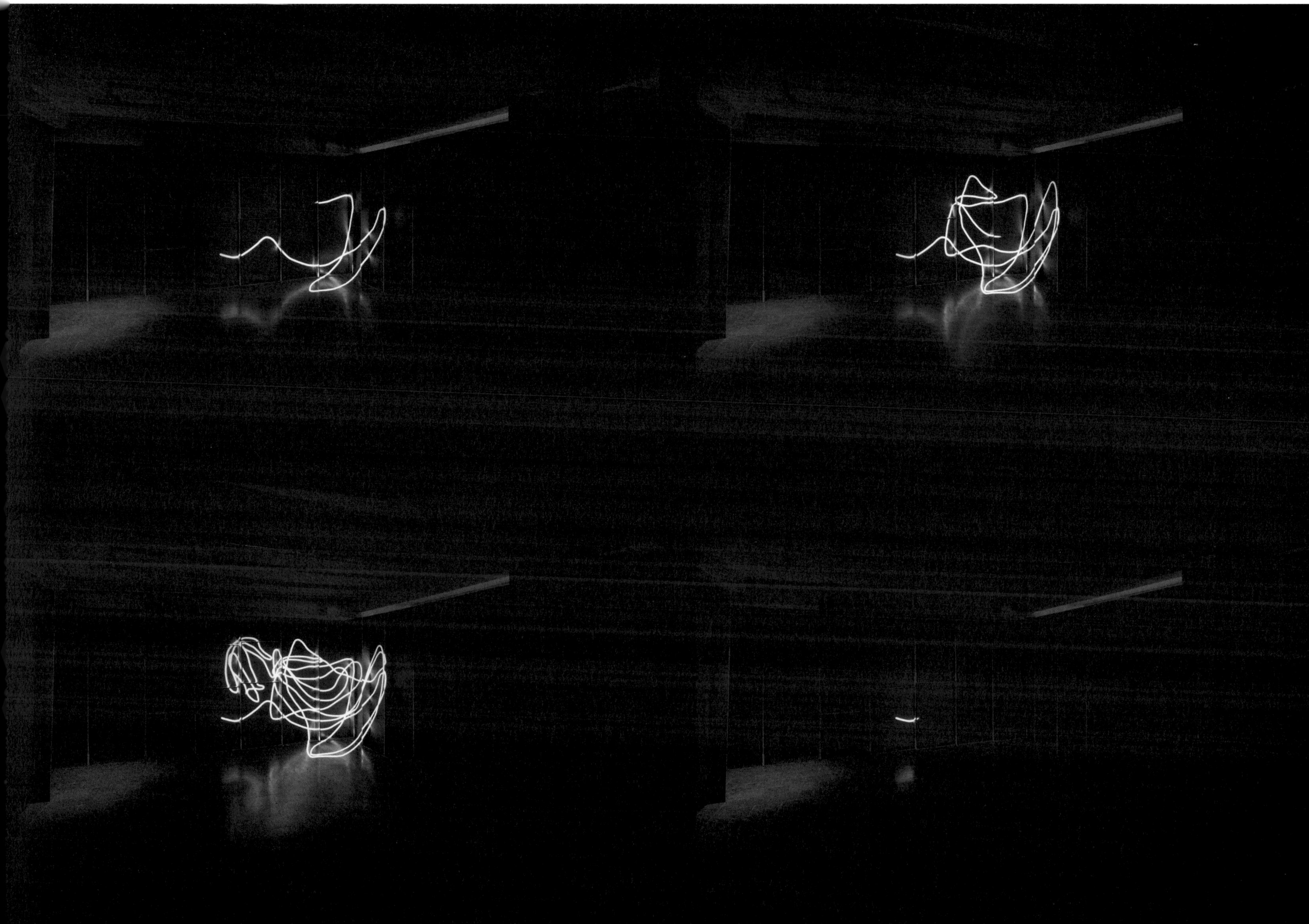

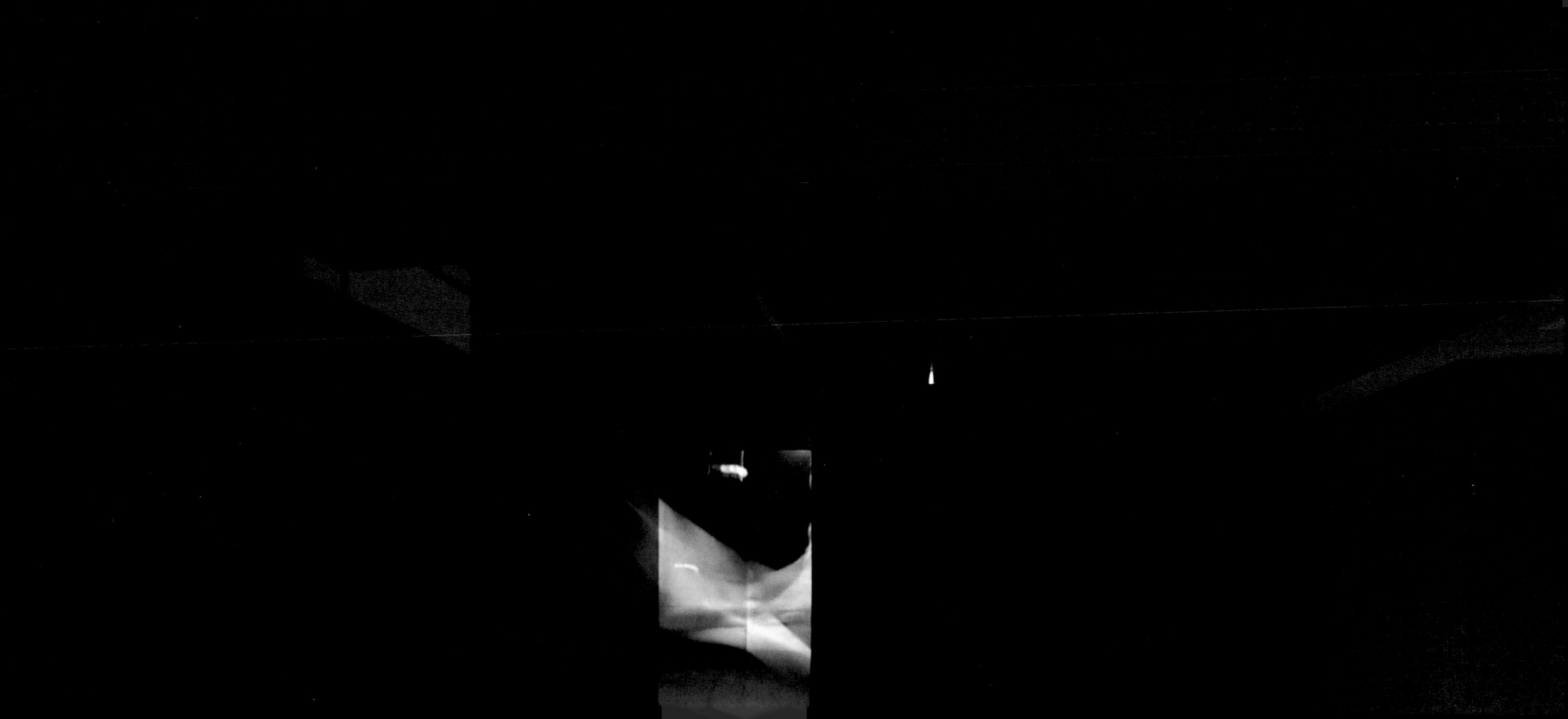

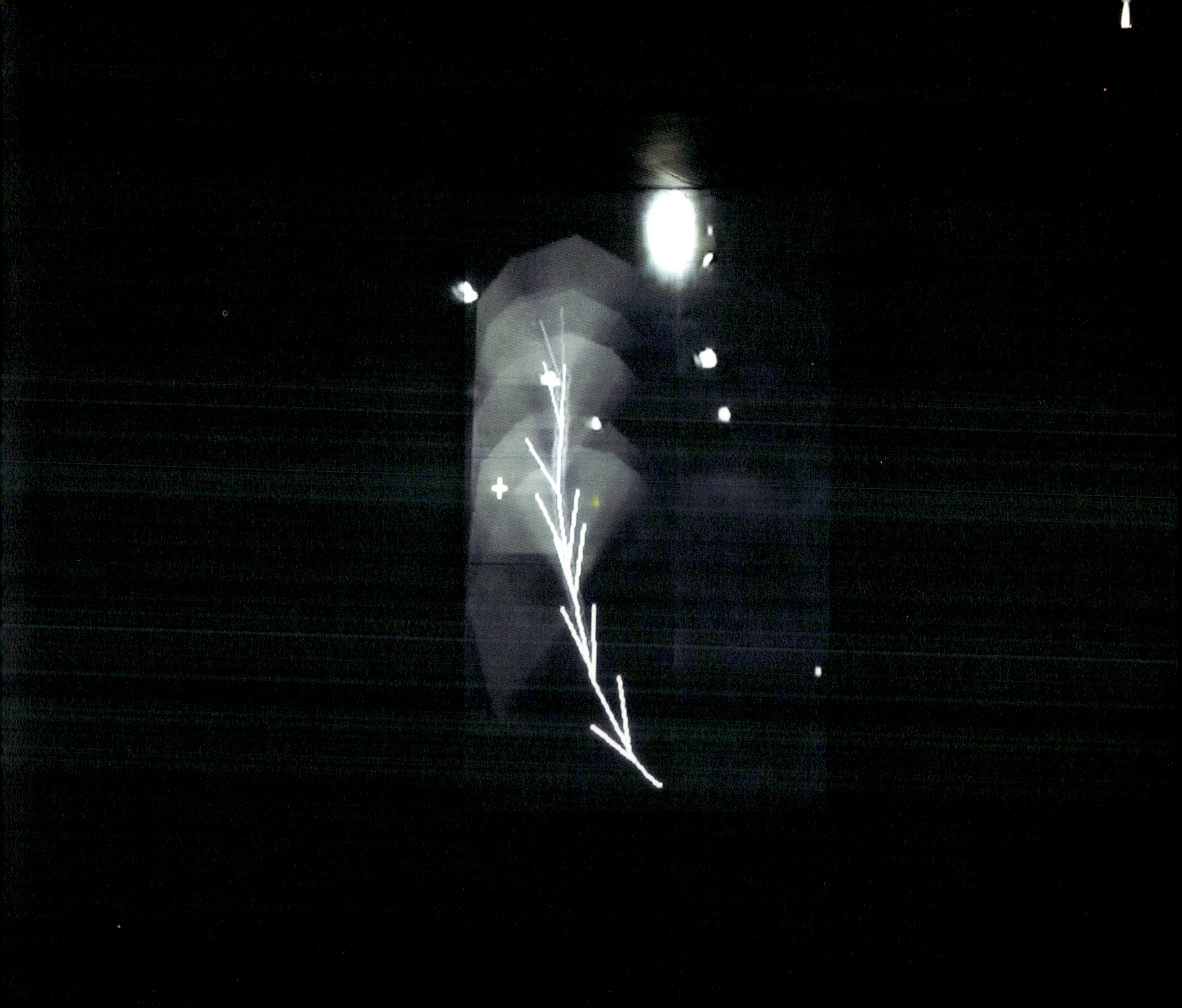

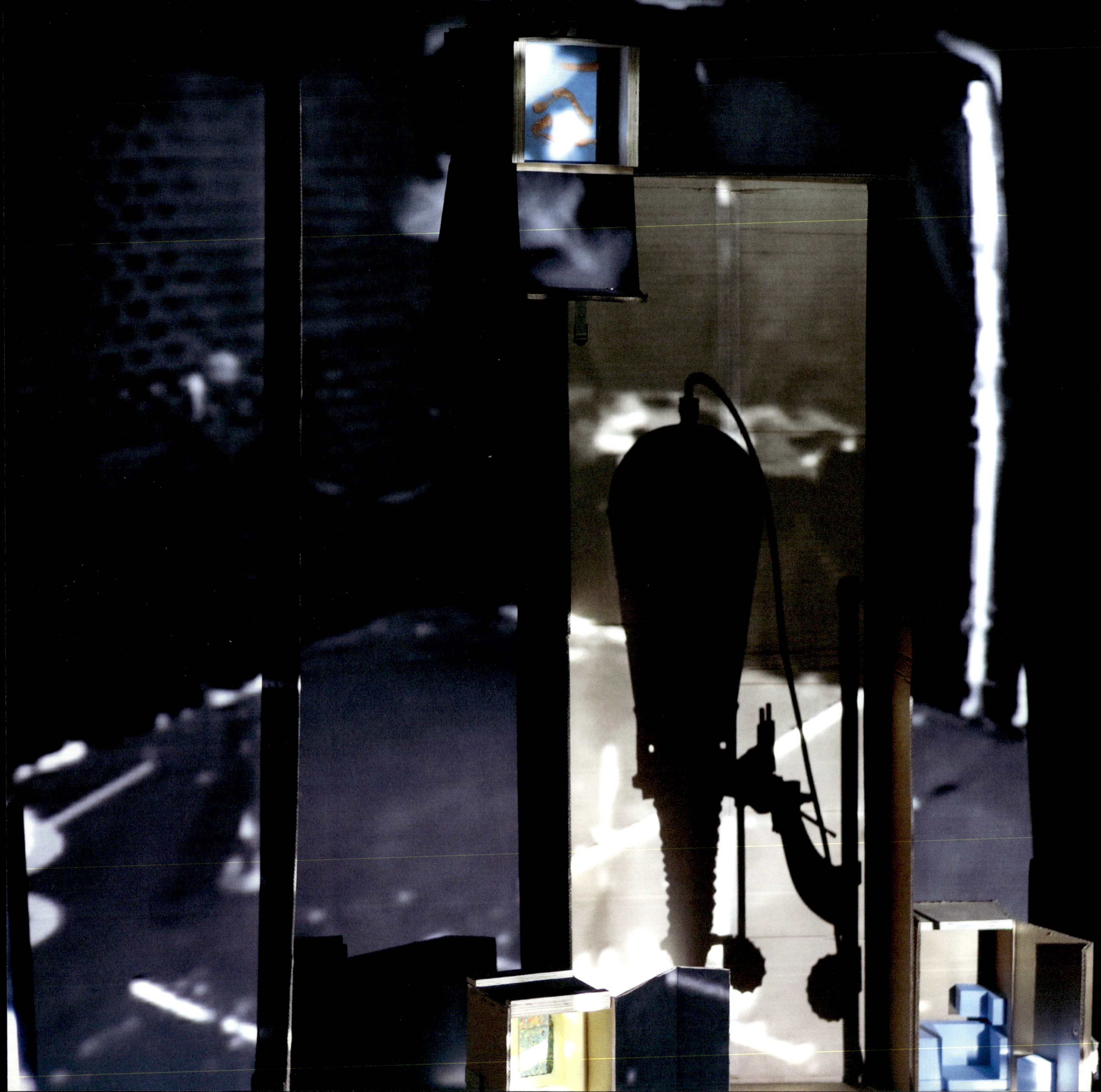

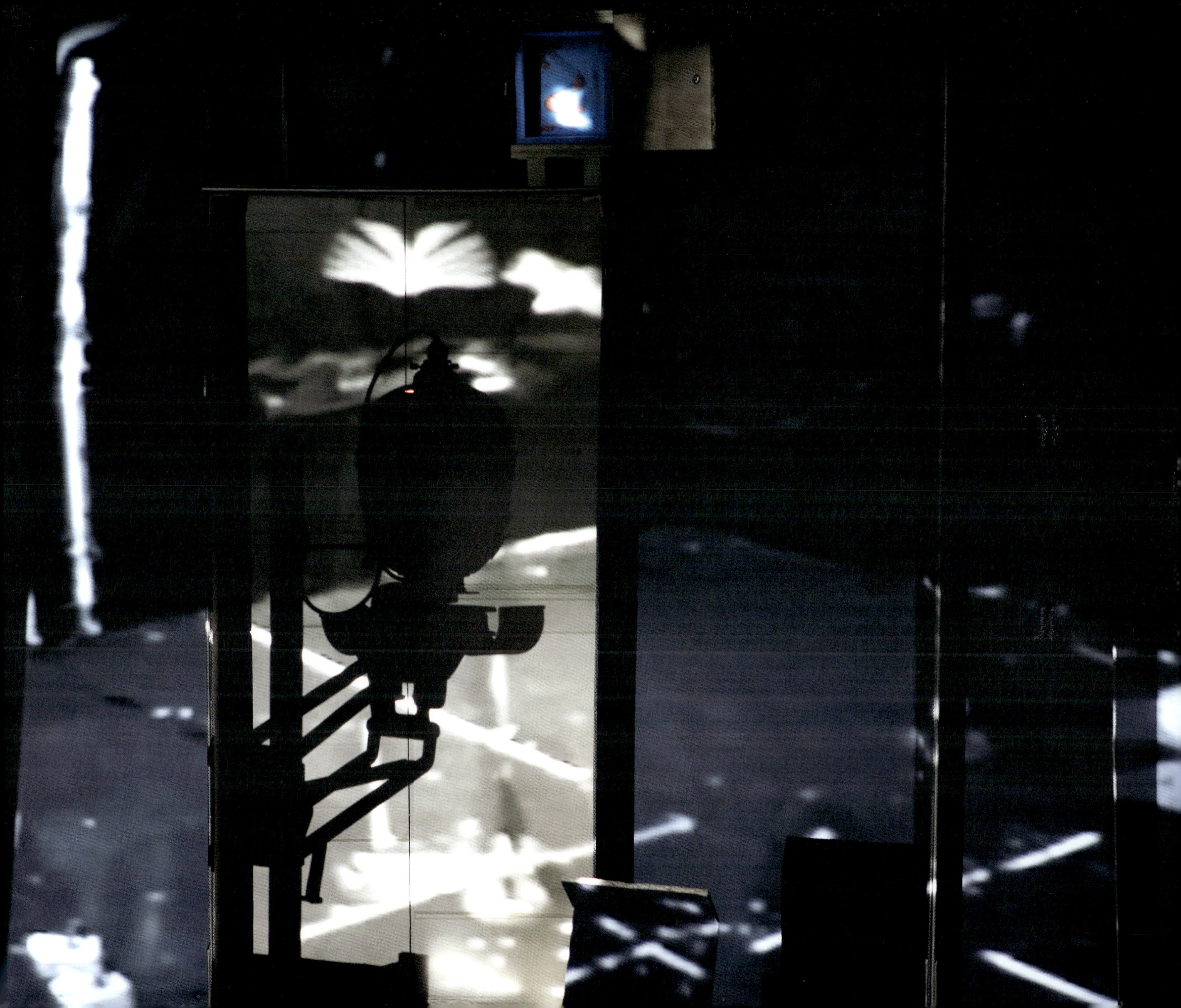

PENNY HES YASSOUR: THE MIND IS A BEAUTIFUL MUSEUM

GALIA BAR OR

"The mind is a beautiful museum
Curated with absent ghosts
Travelling through the imagination
And through its films of dust
And light."
MEIR AGASSI, 1995

THE EPHEMERAL MUSEUM

Meir Agassi's poem wanders through landscapes of transformation in a journey through the spaces of an ephemeral museum: the mind is a beautiful museum.

The mind as museum was a common trope during the early days of museums, about three hundred years ago, a time still rich in sources of inspiration later to be suppressed by the Enlightenment. The Kunstkammer, an early version of the museum, was perceived as a dynamic space, similar to the camera obscura's moving images. Laden with collections, the Kunstkammer was often considered analogous to the mind: an installation of a collection, a visual representation of memory, allying for the working of the mind and enabling discourse. Circular representations of naturalia and artificilia were installed to induce the creation of ever more possibilities of dynamic relationships, just like the human mind. The dynamic

PENNY HES YASSOUR: DER VERSTAND IST EIN SCHÖNES MUSEUM

GALIA BAR OR

„Der Verstand ist ein schönes Museum,
das von abwesenden Geistern kuratiert wird.
Er wandert durch die Fantasie,
die angesammelten Staubschichten
und das Licht."
MEIR AGASSI, 1995

DAS EPHEMERE MUSEUM

Meir Agassis Gedicht wandelt durch sich verändernde Landschaften, es schildert gleichsam eine Reise durch die Räume eines ephemeren Museums: „Der Verstand ist ein schönes Museum".
Als Museen vor ungefähr dreihundert Jahren entstanden, wurden sie oft mit dem Verstand verglichen. Diese Zeit war noch reich an Inspirationsquellen, die später durch die Aufklärung unterdrückt werden sollten. Die Kunstkammer, eine Vorläuferin des Museums, wurde als dynamischer Raum aufgefasst, ähnlich den bewegten Bildern einer Camera obscura. Mit Sammlungsobjekten gefüllt, dienten Kunstkammern häufig als Analogie für den Verstand: Die Einrichtung einer Sammlung und die visuelle Darstellung der Erinnerung verbündeten sich, um die Gedanken zu schärfen und den Diskurs anzuregen. Man begann, Naturalien und Artefakte so zu präsentieren, dass man sie umgehen konnte, um stets neue Möglich-

Kunstkammer pointed also to a utopian perception of society, as seen in the work of Francis Bacon, who described a huge Kunstkammer at the very heart of his utopian society. Bacon also included in his description a mobile "automata," which expands the knowledge of the causes and uncovers the secret nature of the dynamics of things. A distant memory of these concepts is being echoed in the rooms created by Penny Hes Yassour for her exhibition, *Temp-Est*, where it seems that time does not stand still.

The exhibition at the Kunsthalle Recklinghausen is located in a building that originally had been constructed as a bunker intending to protect those caught in the nearby train station during an air raid in World War II. In this massive structure, Hes Yassour built inner rooms from cardboard boxes and plywood. The use of everyday, perishable material gives a sense of ephemerality to the spaces, imbuing them with vulnerable presence within the concrete structure, like some kind of a skull that protects a fragile living tissue.

Penny Hes Yassour filled her constructed chambers with objects that were removed from their original context: pieces of furniture, remnants of architectural models, objects taken from everyday life, scientific tools, old scales once used in labs, and devices for measuring time, mass, and space. At the installation *a·ban·don·ment*, scales transformed into pendulums, which are still moving as if they were indeed ghosts of a Kunstkammer's "automata." Onto the layered formation of her installations, Hes Yassour projected landscapes—natural and cultural—some of which were filmed in the artist's immediate surroundings and others taken from videos that document experiments in research laboratories.

Resonance Towers – between Memory and Oblivion: Within the sealed structure of the Kunsthalle Recklinghausen, landscapes of motion echo one another, reverberating collective and private psychological states and invoking hidden conclaves of a remembrance as worlds within worlds. The movies and the sound reactivate the space, reanimate it with the body's breath and heartbeat, which results in a growing sense of fear perpetuated by an uncanny noise from an unrecognizable outside, comprised of both passion and anxiety.

Penny Hes Yassour's four installations are revealed for the first time in this exhibition. She started work on these installations in 2017 and completed the last installation shortly before the exhibition's opening. The show exposes a new phase and a significant new layer of her art: the works were inspired by her recent encounter with researchers at the Weizmann Institute of Science in Rechovot and the Alexander Silberman Institute of Life Sciences at the Hebrew University of Jerusalem, whom she met when she was invited by the university to be an artist-in-residence. The new artworks integrate her long engagement with the concept of the mental map and the environmental image and the research on cells' processing sensory input in the brain to which she was exposed during her residency.

keiten für dynamische Beziehungen zu schaffen, genau wie beim menschlichen Verstand. Zudem verwies die dynamische Kunstkammer auf das Idealbild einer Gesellschaft, etwa in den Schriften von Francis Bacon, der eine riesige Kunstkammer im Zentrum seiner idealen Gesellschaft beschrieb. Bei Bacon kommt ein beweglicher „Automat" vor, der das Wissen über die Ursachen erweitert und die verborgene Natur der Dynamik der Dinge enthüllt. Die von Penny Hes Yassour in der Ausstellung *Temp-Est* geschaffenen Räume erinnern entfernt daran; auch hier scheint es so, als würde die Zeit nicht stillstehen. Die Ausstellung der Kunsthalle Recklinghausen wurde in einem ursprünglich als Bunker errichteten Gebäude installiert, das während des Zweiten Weltkriegs all jenen Schutz bieten sollte, die im nahe gelegenen Bahnhof von einem Luftangriff überrascht wurden. In diesen massiven Baukörper setzte Hes Yassour mit Karton und Sperrholz innere Räume. Das alltägliche, begrenzt haltbare Material lässt diese Räume vergänglich wirken, wie eine verletzliche Präsenz innerhalb der Betonstruktur, die sie umschließt wie ein Schädel, der ebenfalls eine fragile, lebendige Gewebestruktur schützt.

Die Räume füllte Penny Hes Yassour mit Gegenständen, die sie ihrem ursprünglichen Kontext entnommen hatte: Möbelstücke, Reste von Architekturmodellen, alltägliche Objekte, wissenschaftliche Instrumente, alte, ausrangierte Laborwaagen und Geräte zur Zeit-, Mengen- und Raummessung. Die Installation *a·ban·don·ment* zeigt zu Pendeln umgewandelte Waagen, die sich noch immer bewegen, als wären sie tatsächlich Geister eines aus einer Kunstkammer stammenden „Automaten". Auf die vielschichtige Struktur ihrer Installationen projizierte Hes Yassour natürliche und kulturelle Landschaften. Einige davon wurden in der unmittelbaren Umgebung der Künstlerin gefilmt, während andere Videos die Experimente in Forschungslaboren dokumentieren.

Resonance Towers – between Memory and Oblivion: Im Inneren des fensterlosen Baus der Kunsthalle Recklinghausen bilden Bewegungslandschaften ein gegenseitiges Echo aus – das Nachhallen kollektiver und individueller Seelenzustände, die verborgene Konklaven der Erinnerung als Welten innerhalb von Welten wachrufen. Die Filme und der Ton reaktivieren den Raum; sie verleihen ihm neues Leben wie der Atem und Herzschlag einem Körper. Das erweckt ein sich steigerndes Angstgefühl, eine Mischung aus Leidenschaft und Sorge, ausgelöst durch den unheimlichen Lärm von einem nicht erkennbaren Außenraum.

Die vier Installationen Hes Yassours werden in dieser Ausstellung zum ersten Mal gezeigt. Sie begann 2017 an ihnen zu arbeiten und schloss die letzte Installation kurz vor der Eröffnung ab. So gibt die Ausstellung Einblick in eine neue Phase und eine bedeutende neue Ebene ihrer Kunst: Die Werke wurden von ihren jüngsten Begegnungen mit Forschern des Weizmann Institute of Science in Rechovot und des Alexander Silberman Institute of Life Sciences der Hebräischen Universität Jerusalem angeregt, als sie dort Artist in Residence war. In diese Kunstwerke floss ihre lange Beschäftigung

The opening poem by Meir Agassi and the image of the dynamic Kunstkammer as a metaphor for the mind are charged with new meaning in the context of Hes Yassour's current work.

Meir Agassi wrote about Hes Yassour's early mental map art: the information stored within her mental maps stands in stark contradiction to the information of the cartographic map, which is useful and is supposed to take us somewhere. Hes Yassour's map might just take us to our inner labyrinth, a place which is a non-place, entirely unmarked and undocumented.[1]

MENTAL MAPS

When Hes Yassour started working as a student within Regional Geography (Haifa University), the field was still young and innovative. Its interdisciplinary nature offered a critical mode of interrogation that was not only fertile but also ethical for the evolving field of geography, which in the nineteen-seventies was rather restricted. Her research there focused on the mental map and the environmental image. Hes Yassour embedded her findings into her artistic practice in an attempt to create more complex formations of visual representations as well as multidisciplinary installations.

The mental image may be defined as the total subjective images of the external physical world. It is constructed from a set of symbols and representations carried by individuals and groups. The mental map, on the other hand, is affected and formed by tendencies, experiences, memories, thinking habits, life patterns, spatial orientations, ideologies, and politics. A mental map is current and dynamic by its very nature—and even if its visual manifestations are subjective, there are essential components in its design influenced by the various types of cartography. But unlike the formal cartographic map, which homogenizes diverse spatial narratives and obliterates traces of human experience, the mental map subverts what purports to be "an objective instance" and enables the action of flexible approaches.

Hes Yassour implemented an interdisciplinary approach while not only using a variety of disciplines, such as science, geology, architecture, and psychoanalysis, among others. She also used a variety of media and materials of diverse sources spanning the military industry to materials she developed herself for her specific installations.

Viewed as a whole, the work resists any total system of seemingly objective "truth" while remaining alert to the gap between reality and its representations. Her spatial installations aim at breaking the continuum, expanding the fringes, challenging what is considered "significant," and turning absence into presence.

mit der „Mental Map“, der kognitiven Landkarte, und dem Bild der Umwelt ein, genauso wie die Forschung über Sinneseindrücke verarbeitende Gehirnzellen, von denen sie während ihres Aufenthaltsstipendiums erfahren hatte.
Das Eröffnungsgedicht von Meir Agassi und das Bild der dynamischen Kunstkammer als Metapher für den Verstand erlangen im Kontext von Hes Yassours aktueller Arbeit eine neue Bedeutung. Meir Agassi schreibt über Hes Yassours frühe Werke zu kognitiven Landkarten, dass diese Informationen enthalten, die in krassem Widerspruch zu den in kartografischen Karten verzeichneten Angaben stehen. Letztere sind nützlich und sollen uns zu einem Ziel führen. Hes Yassours Karte führt uns höchstens zu unserem inneren Labyrinth, zu einem Ort, der eigentlich keiner ist, völlig ungekennzeichnet und undokumentiert.[1]

KOGNITIVE LANDKARTEN

Als Penny Hes Yassour während ihres Studiums an der Universität Haifa begann, sich mit dem Bereich der Länderkunde zu beschäftigen, war dieses Feld noch ganz neu und innovativ. Der interdisziplinäre Ansatz eignete sich für die kritische Hinterfragung, die sich für die Entwicklung des Fachs Geografie (das in den 1970er-Jahren sehr eingeschränkt war) als fruchtbar und ethisch richtig erwies. Hes Yassours Forschung konzentrierte sich auf die kognitive Landkarte und das Bild der Umwelt. Die Ergebnisse verarbeitete sie in ihren Kunstwerken, mit dem Ziel, komplexere Strukturen visueller Darstellungen und interdisziplinäre Installationen zu schaffen.
Das geistige Bild kann als die Summe aller subjektiven Bilder der externen, physischen Welt definiert werden. Es setzt sich aus einer Reihe von Symbolen und Darstellungen zusammen, die Einzelpersonen und Gruppen mit sich tragen. Die kognitive Landkarte wird dagegen durch Neigungen, Erfahrungen, Erinnerungen, Denkgewohnheiten, Lebensmuster, räumliche Orientierungen, Ideologien und Politik beeinflusst und geformt. Sie ist von Natur aus aktuell und dynamisch – und auch wenn ihre visuellen Manifestationen subjektiv sind, gibt es wesentliche Komponenten ihrer Gestaltung, die in gewisser Weise von der Kartografie beeinflusst wurden. Aber im Gegensatz zur formal kartografischen Karte, die verschiedene räumliche Erzählungen homogenisiert und Spuren menschlicher Erfahrung auslöscht, untergräbt die kognitive Landkarte das, was vorgibt, eine „objektive Instanz“ zu sein und ermöglicht flexible Ansätze.
Hes Yassour geht interdisziplinär vor, indem sie nicht nur aus verschiedenen Disziplinen – Naturwissenschaft, Geologie, Architektur, Psychoanalyse und so weiter – schöpft, sondern auch eine Vielfalt von Medien und Werkstoffen aus

Some of the poetic titles of her installations comprise duplicated spaces, which allude to the duplications that entail the existence of a hidden doppelganger. At times, the double is the space itself rather than a figure as implied; for instance, in *Space and its Double – Observations* or *The UnseenScene*. Some of the words in her textual works lend themselves to utter unreadability, and the unseen words float in a vacuum, like a scene that is merely implied rather than being fully articulated. The antagonistic element is ever present, even in a system supposedly absolute and resolved, bursting forth through the uncontrollable and the obsessive.

MENTAL MAPS – PRODUCTION HALLS

The *unheimlich* (uncanny) is evoked at the most rational places, in the supposedly well-ordered and clear space. As early as the nineteen-nineties, Hes Yassour focused on and explored systems that force a rationale of a strict and total space that neuters and blocks the temporary element leaving almost no trace. Her work distinctly dealt with the way that the bunker sutures structures of ambivalence that are, on the one hand, defensive and reclusive but could easily transform into a trap. The archetype of the bunker is a priori associated to an individual or a collective response to a psychological threat, its role already dual: both an offshoot of aggression as well as self-blocking reclusiveness, which could be local and global and today appears to be even more relevant than before. The bunker serves also as a blueprint for the notion of spatial expansion. A constituent exhibition in this sense was entitled *Mental Maps – Production Halls*, installed at the Mishkan Museum of Art, Ein Harod (1993). Whereas within the confines of Recklinghausen Hes Yassour created vulnerable rooms from cardboard and plywood, in Ein Harod she created a firm, almost totalitarian space. In both cases, she created a counterpoint to the building's structure. The Mishkan Museum is known for its windowed ceilings that provide indirect natural light and for its thin walls. In its illuminated and fragile architecture, she built a sort of production hall that morphs between the concrete and the imaginary. She blocked the natural light in the hall and illuminated it with the cold light of a row of elongated fluorescent lamps hanging from the ceiling, hanging low over

Mental Maps – Production Halls, Mishkan Museum of Art, Ein Harod, 1993

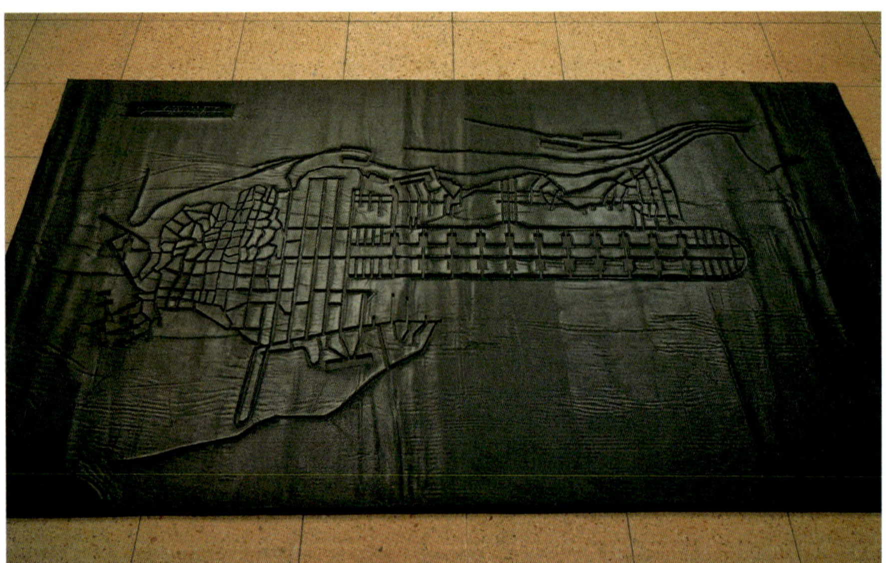

unterschiedlichen Quellen einbezieht, die von der Militärausrüstung bis hin zu Materialien reichen, die sie eigens für ihre Installationen entwickelt.

Als Ganzes betrachtet, entzieht sich ihr Werk einer scheinbar objektiven „Wahrheit“, behält aber ein Gespür für die Kluft zwischen Wirklichkeit und der Darstellung von Wirklichkeit. Ziel ihrer Rauminstallationen ist, das Kontinuum zu durchbrechen, die Ränder auszudehnen, das infrage zu stellen, was als „bedeutend“ angesehen wird und Abwesenheit in Anwesenheit zu verwandeln.

Die poetischen Titel einiger ihrer Installationen spielen auf die Vervielfältigung von Räumen an, die ihrerseits auf die Existenz eines verborgenen Doppelgängers hinweist. Manchmal ist keine Figur, sondern der Raum selbst die Verdopplung, wie im Fall von *Space and its Double – Observations* und *The UnseenScene.* In ihren Arbeiten mit Text sind einige Worte unlesbar, sie schweben unsichtbar in einem Vakuum, wie eine Szene, die nur angedeutet und nicht ausformuliert wird. Das antagonistische Element ist immer präsent, selbst in einem angeblich absoluten und gelösten System – es tritt durch das Unkontrollierbare und Zwanghafte hervor.

MENTAL MAPS – PRODUCTION HALLS

Das Unheimliche wird an Orten beschworen, wo scheinbar die Vernunft regiert, in vermeintlich geregelten und übersichtlichen Räumen. Bereits in den 1990er-Jahren konzentrierte sich Penny Hes Yassour auf die Erforschung des Grundprinzips eines strikten und absoluten Raums, der das Zeitgefühl hemmt und ausschaltet, sodass es fast keine Spuren hinterlässt. In ihrem Werk setzt sie sich eingehend damit auseinander, auf welche Weise der Bunker ambivalente Merkmale in sich vereint, indem er einerseits als Schutzraum und Rückzugsort dient, sich andererseits aber leicht in eine Falle verwandeln kann. Das Urbild des Bunkers wird a priori mit einer individuellen oder kollektiven Reaktion auf eine psychologische Bedrohung verbunden. Er hat eine Doppelrolle, als eine Folge von Aggression und einer sich selbst einschließenden Zurückgezogenheit, die lokal oder global sein kann und heute sogar noch wichtiger erscheint als früher. Der Bunker dient auch als Plan für die Vorstellung von räumlicher Expansion.

Diesem Thema widmete sich eine Ausstellung mit dem Titel *Mental Maps – Production Halls,* die 1993 am Mishkan Museum of Art in Ein Harod zu sehen war. Während Hes Yassour in dem massiv gebauten Raummantel von Recklinghausen zerbrechliche Räume aus Karton und Sperrholz schuf, errichtete sie in Ein Harod robuste, fast totalitäre Räume. In beiden

large, massive wooden structures, perhaps work tables that may well be shelters. On the huge tables, she placed maps—including an architectural floor plan for a German bunker used to produce ammunition during World War II—embedded in rubber-silicone surfaces, using a dark green material, resistant to fire, water, or pressure. In order to work with this material, which was unknown outside the military industry, she collaborated with an aircraft manufacturer. Using gaps and shifts in relation to the body, she disrupted the body's experience and the spatial logic. In addressing the issue of the manner in which a spatial pattern carries within it information and a social meaning, she used sculptural and spatial-temporal relations, as well as documents, maps, and blueprints. These historical schematics, embedded in a different material, essentially projected the inner logic of the space-time relationship at the moment of their creation. Jean-François Chevrier identified the contradiction of forces at work in her installation *Mental Maps – Production Halls*: "The ensemble defines a complex space, rigid but disarticulated, distributed over several levels and suffused with emptiness."[2] The concepts imbued form a sculptural language that phrases the fictional, border-lined dimension of space, creating a disturbing imbalance between a massive-solid appearance and spatial emptiness. Thus Hes Yassour disrupts the extreme circumstance of absoluteness and systemic strictness using spatial gaps and shifts, and while excising the monument concept of meaning, she is still using its gestures.

SPATIAL, FICTIONAL, PERFORMATIVE

Contrary to the idea of the seemingly independent objective-mathematical space, spatiality occurs through and by the presence of a subject. Both conceptual and phenomenological, spatiality is part of human existence; namely, a subjective perception of the complex positions and arrangements of components in relation to both body and environment. Through the exploration of spatiality, Hes Yassour's installations seem to increase viewer participation, the "audience's sensorium." The spatial touches the non-verbal bodily experience and emphasizes the attentiveness to elements such as materiality and temporality, space and place. By confronting the unfamiliar and the non-narrative complexity, the spatial is thus challenging perceptions and conventions of representation.

But one of the important features of spatiality is temporality and change, and with it comes the awareness for the fragility of memory. It inevitably hangs on a kind of entrapment, for Hes Yassour's installations often include camouflage and a complex hanging network of texts and traces of landscapes—but that is another story. On the other hand, her work ostensibly

Fällen setzte sie einen Kontrapunkt zur Struktur des umgebenden Baus. Das Mishkan Museum of Art ist bekannt für seine Oberlichtfenster, durch die indirektes, natürliches Licht von oben einfällt, sowie für seine dünnen Wände. In dieser zarten und lichtdurchfluteten Architektur errichtete Hes Yassour eine Art Produktionshalle, die zwischen dem Konkreten und dem Imaginären changierte. Sie unterband den natürlichen Lichteinfall und beleuchtete den Raum stattdessen mit dem kalten Licht einer Reihe von an der Decke befestigten Leuchtstoffröhren, die knapp über großen, massiven Holzplatten hingen – möglicherweise Werkbänken, die aber auch als Unterschlupf hätten dienen können. Auf die großen Platten legte sie neben Landkarten auch den Grundriss eines deutschen Bunkers, in dem während des Zweiten Weltkriegs Munition hergestellt worden war. Für die Karten verwendete sie ein dunkelgrünes Kautschukmaterial, das gegen Feuer, Wasser und Druck resistent ist. Um mit diesem außerhalb der Militärindustrie unbekannten Material umgehen zu können, arbeitete sie mit einem Flugzeughersteller zusammen. Lücken und Verschiebungen setzte sie gezielt ein, um die Erfahrung des Körpers und die räumliche Logik zu stören. Bei der Auseinandersetzung mit der Frage, inwieweit eine Raumstruktur Informationen und soziale Bedeutung in sich trägt, nutzte sie skulpturale und räumlich-zeitliche Beziehungen wie auch Dokumente, Landkarten und Entwürfe. Die in einem anderen Material ausgeführten historischen Pläne sind im Grunde eine Projektion der Logik der Raum-Zeit-Beziehung im Moment ihrer Entstehung. Jean-François Chevrier identifizierte die in der Installation *Mental Maps – Production Halls* einander widersprechenden Kräfte: „Das Ensemble zeichnet einen komplexen Raum nach, der starr, aber fragmentiert und über mehrere Ebenen verteilt ist und völlig leer wirkt.“[2]

In ihren Konzepten entwickelt die Künstlerin eine skulpturale Sprache, welche die fiktive, grenzwertige Dimension des Raums formuliert und ein verstörendes Ungleichgewicht zwischen der massiven Erscheinung und räumlichen Leere schafft. Hes Yassour durchbricht die Extreme von Absolutheit und systemischer Strenge, indem sie räumliche Lücken und Verschiebungen nutzt, und obwohl sie die ursprüngliche Bedeutung des Denkmals ausblendet, setzt sie dessen Ausdruckssprache für sich ein.

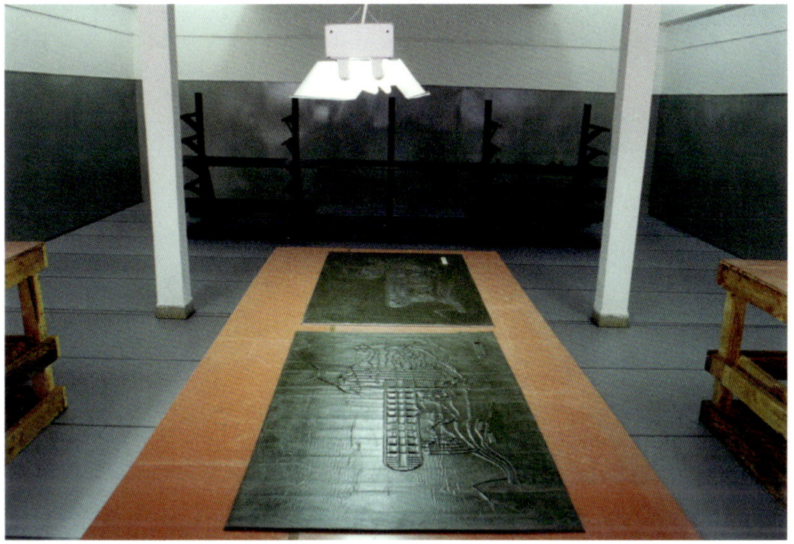

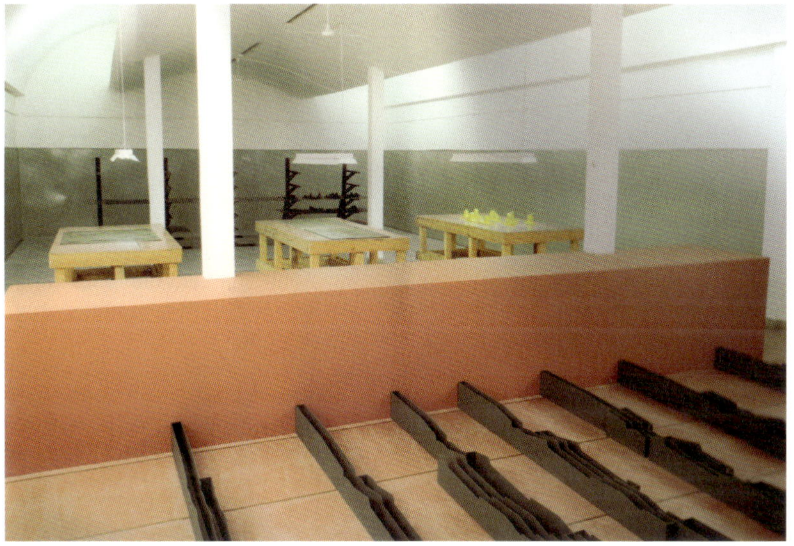

Mental Maps – Production Halls,
Mishkan Museum of Art, Ein Harod, 1993

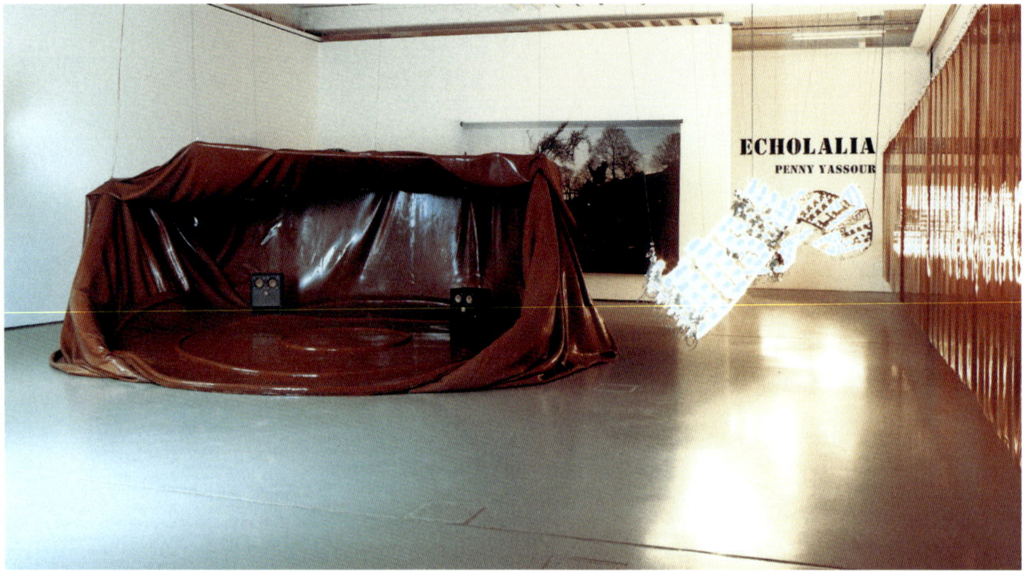

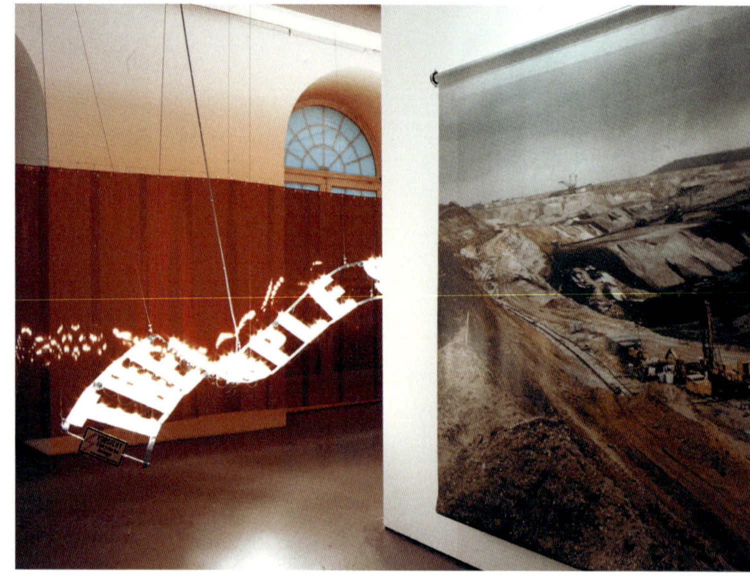

Echolalia, Kasseler Kunstverein, Fridericianum, Kassel, 2000/01

relates to the necessity to demarcate unconventional ways to invoke remembrance. Spatiality may invoke a kind of theatricality that borders a liminal space capable of articulating the relation between alterity and fiction, "a space of otherness." Following her participation in the 10th documenta in Kassel, in 1997, Hes Yassour received the Arnold Bode Award for her work *Mental Maps – Involuntary Memory* and was invited to exhibit at the Fridericianum in Kassel. She created the exhibition *Echolalia*,[3] in which she "choreographed" an interactive sound-image assemblage, structured as a path of a poetic text: "I had a night dream: The people swarmed on the public square, and pointed laughingly at me, and I was filled with shame and fear." The text was loaded with an involuntary memory that carried biographical, fictional, and historical dimensions. A multi-channeled sound and music piece was composed by Haim Permont and integrated as a significant integral part of the installation. It was played through tiny microphones placed along the path and at the adjacent sculptural structures. One of them was *Soft Arena*, a soft rubber structure that looked like a round stage, or a huge gaping mouth, where a female singer's voice was heard reflecting on the nightmarish experience. Next to it, the sound of a wild gathering crowd was heard. A spiral path of letters, illuminated by incandescent light bulbs, made up the last section of the exhibition: "and I was filled with shame and fear."

RÄUMLICH, FIKTIV, PERFORMATIV

Im Gegensatz zum scheinbar unabhängigen, objektiven und mathematischen Raum entsteht Räumlichkeit durch die Anwesenheit eines Subjekts. Räumlichkeit gehört konzeptionell und phänomenologisch zur menschlichen Existenz, nämlich als eine subjektive Auffassung von komplexen Positionen und Anordnungen von Komponenten in Bezug auf den Körper und die Umgebung. Durch die Erforschung der Räumlichkeit scheinen Penny Hes Yassours Installationen die Beteiligung der Betrachter – das „Sensorium des Publikums" – zu steigern. Das Räumliche wirkt mit der nonverbalen, körperlichen Erfahrung zusammen und betont die Beachtung von Elementen wie Materialität und Zeitlichkeit, Raum und Ort. Durch die Gegenüberstellung des Ungewohnten und der nicht narrativen Komplexität stellt das Räumliche die Wahrnehmung und Konvention der Wiedergabe infrage.

Zeitlichkeit und Wandel sind wichtige Merkmale der Räumlichkeit, die auch ein Bewusstsein für die Fragilität der Erinnerung mit sich bringen. Unweigerlich hängt das mit einer Art „Falle" zusammen, da in Hes Yassours Installationen oft Camouflage und ein komplexes, schwebendes Netzwerk von Texten und Landschaftsspuren enthalten sind, aber das ist eine andere Geschichte. Andererseits bezieht sich Hes Yassours Werk scheinbar auf die Notwendigkeit, unkonventionelle Wege aufzuzeigen, um Erinnerung wachzurufen. Räumlichkeit mag an eine Art Theatralität denken lassen, die einen Schwellenraum abgrenzt, der in der Lage ist, die Beziehung zwischen Andersartigkeit und Fiktion auszudrücken, „ein Raum des Andersseins".

Hes Yassour nahm 1997 mit ihrem Werk *Mental Maps – Involuntary Memory* an der documenta X in Kassel teil, anschließend erhielt sie den Arnold-Bode-Preis und wurde eingeladen, im Fridericianum auszustellen. Dafür entwickelte sie die Ausstellung *Echolalia,*[3] für die sie eine interaktive Klang-Bild-Assemblage „choreografierte", die wie der Pfad eines poetischen Textes aufgebaut ist: „Eines Nachts hatte ich einen Traum: Auf einem öffentlichen Platz wimmelte es von Leuten, die lachend auf mich zeigten, und ich war von Scham und Angst erfüllt." Der Text war voller unfreiwilliger Erinnerungen, die biografische, fiktive und historische Informationen enthielten. Haim Permont komponierte eine mehrkanalige Klang- und Musikmischung, die ein bedeutender Bestandteil der Installation war. Sie ertönte durch winzige Mikrofone, die entlang des Weges und an den angrenzenden, skulpturalen Strukturen angebracht waren. Dazu gehörte *Soft Arena,* ein weiches Gummigebilde, das wie eine runde Bühne oder ein riesiger, geöffneter Mund aussah, aus dem eine singende Frauenstimme ertönte, die von der albtraumhaften Erfahrung berichtete. Daneben war der Lärm einer wilden Menschenmenge zu hören. Den letzten Abschnitt der Ausstellung bildete ein spiralförmiger, durch Glühbirnen beleuchteter Buchstabenpfad: „and I was filled with shame and fear" (und ich war von Scham und Angst erfüllt).

Soft Arena was described by the artist as "psycho-physical architecture: a theater as a body and the body as a theater." The complex performed nightmare carried biographical concealed inlets, for only after the exhibition did Hes Yassour's grandfather's story come to light. His ancestors came from the Hessen region, and the name is still part of the artist's identity via her second name, Hes. *Echolalia* turned out to be an echo of indeed an involuntary and transgenerational memory in the form of a biographical/historical story that has never been told, as if life were imitating art. Unexpectedly, the facts were revealed after the exhibition ended, and it seems that Hes Yassour explored from the start of her work as an artist spatial-fictional-performative possibilities to deal with the complex and layered ways in which dormant collective and private psychological residues resurface through the process of involuntary memory. She often invoked grotesque images, situations, and sites of performative structures, such as an amusement park, a festival, a parade, or a theater. She also dealt with the Theater of Memory associated, as is known, with the Kunstkammer world—another performative rendition, albeit obsolete, of a mental map of memory, which also serves as a reference to one of the rooms in the exhibition in Recklinghausen.

ERODED LANDSCAPES

Every single exhibition by Penny Hess Yassour is an event and a world unto its own, linked to deep veins throughout her work and opening up new horizons of modes of expression and layers of meaning. Her identity as an artist is not based on a specific medium, theme, or style; all of her exhibitions may be seen as site specific installations.

The Recklinghausen exhibition is built like a labyrinth of new audio-visual assemblages. The artist's description of one of her installations in the exhibition sheds light on significant emphases for her and her work—the installation was inspired by the bats' laboratory at the Neurobiology Department of the Weizmann Institute of Science.

Space and its Double – Observations is an installation of spaces within spaces; each is a spatial-sensory array, reflected as in a mirror side by side, as if similar but slightly different. The imaginary paths construct a rhythm of motion, breath, and sound, like theatrical figures. The flying spiral movement is projected into space and cuts through objects and surfaces at varying depths, revealing or canceling the sequence of movements and pointing to the way the spatial memory is constructed, partial and incomplete, a Theater of Memory. Thus the darkroom/theater is an actual space, spread with light lines of flight and sound; once again the spaces transform and reflect an autonomous new audio-visual language. The ref-

Die Künstlerin beschrieb *Soft Arena* als „eine psycho-physische Architektur: ein Theater als Körper und der Körper als ein Theater“. Der komplex vorgeführte Albtraum enthielt versteckte biografische Einfügungen, denn die Geschichte von Hes Yassours Großvater wurde erst nach der Ausstellung bekannt. Seine Vorfahren stammten aus Hessen, was noch immer Teil der Identität der Künstlerin ist, worauf ihr zweiter Name, Hes, hindeutet. *Echolalia* stellte sich als Widerhall einer unfreiwilligen und generationsübergreifenden Erinnerung heraus, eine biografisch-historische Geschichte, die noch nie zuvor erzählt worden war, als würde das Leben die Kunst imitieren. Überraschenderweise wurden die Fakten nach Ausstellungsende enthüllt, und es schien, als erforschte Penny Hes Yassour seit dem Beginn ihrer künstlerischen Laufbahn räumliche, fiktive und performative Möglichkeiten, um die komplexen und vielschichtigen Arten zu behandeln, auf die schlummernde kollektive und individuelle psychologische Details durch den Vorgang der unfreiwilligen Erinnerung wieder hervorgebracht werden. Hes Yassour hat sich oft auf groteske Bilder, Situationen und performative Orte berufen, etwa einen Vergnügungspark, ein Festival, eine Parade oder ein Theater. Ebenso befasste sie sich mit dem Theater der Erinnerung, das, wie oben gezeigt, mit der Kunstkammer in Beziehung steht – eine andere performative (wenn auch überholte) Wiedergabe einer kognitiven Landkarte der Erinnerung, die genauso als Bezugspunkt für einen der Räume in der Ausstellung in Recklinghausen dient.

ERODED LANDSCAPES

Jede Ausstellung Hes Yassours ist ein Ereignis und eine Welt für sich, die tief in ihrem Werk verwurzelt ist und neue Ausdrucksmöglichkeiten und Bedeutungsebenen erschließt. Sie lässt sich künstlerisch nicht auf ein bestimmtes Medium, Thema oder einen Stil festlegen, und ihre Arbeiten sind immer ortsspezifische Installationen.

Die Ausstellung *Temp-Est* ist wie ein Labyrinth aus neuen audiovisuellen Elementen zusammengesetzt. In ihrer Beschreibung einer der Installationen gibt die Künstlerin Aufschluss über die Punkte, die ihr wichtig sind. Inspiriert wurde sie zu diesem Werk durch das Fledermauslabor am Fachbereich für Neurobiologie des Weizmann Institute of Science: *Space and its Double – Observations* stellt Räume innerhalb von Räumen dar, von denen jeder eine eigene räumlich-sensorische Ordnung hat; wie Spiegelbilder nebeneinandergestellt, wirken sie ähnlich, aber doch leicht anders. Die imaginären Wege bilden einen Rhythmus aus Bewegung, Atem und Klang, wie Theaterfiguren. Eine fliegende Spiralbewegung greift in den Raum aus und schneidet Objekte und Oberflächen unterschiedlich tief ein. Dabei enthüllt oder löscht sie die Bewe-

erence to the Theater of Memory in the artist's poetic description does not appear to be incidental. This sixteenth-century theater, although it survived in memory by no more than a fragmentary text, continues to stir the imagination in the desire to create an ultimate scheme of memory. It is perceived as a fascinating pioneering effort to represent the memory network using links between the spatial and the performative: the space has a graded structure (like an amphitheater), and the grading has a hierarchical and categorical significance. Mythological figures stand on the steps and reactivate a complex network of affinities and internal relations.

Hes Yassour's reference to the Theatre of Memory is meaningful, since the language she has developed over the years in her installation works is unique and innovative in these two significant dimensions: the spatial dimension and the performative.

Through them she explores spatial patterns that project a structure of relationships, memory, and forgetfulness, including an implicit expression of present time.

The spatial and the performative weave anew the layered network of contexts and expressions in each exhibition.

In the Recklinghausen exhibition, which includes sound and projections, she creates four spatial installations, each appearing to be part research lab, part collection room, or perhaps theater stage. They are interwoven with pieces of material and pictorial memory and the resonance of current time along with recollections associated with disciplines in which she worked independently as an artist-researcher.

In the description by Hes Yassour, the Theatre of Memory is also mentioned, in a reflexive context that resonates in the depth of her work as an artist.

Reflexive art deals with the question of the very essence of art making and traces the place of art as a language and its modes of operation as a transformation.

The reflexive dimension is alluded to in almost all of her images and contexts: a mental map, or a museum which is both brain and mind, and the installation inspired by the bat research lab that she mentions in her description, transforming into an autonomous audio-visual language.

As noted above, the mental map context is a constitutive element in her work. That she was exposed "in real time" to the emerging rich discourse of environmental geography as a research student while she was already working as an artist is significant. Contemporary art as well also adopted and subsumed the spatial turn, and further down the line the performative turn (Vito Acconci, Robert Morris). But although in both disciplines the seminal philosophy at this turning point was mainly phenomenalism (Maurice Merleau-Ponty), each of them developed a distinct discourse: Hes Yassour worked in both.

gungsfolge und verweist darauf, wie die räumliche Erinnerung aufgebaut ist: einseitig und unvollständig, ein Theater der Erinnerung. Auf diese Weise ist die Dunkelkammer/das Theater einmal ein wirklicher Raum, durchzogen von Lichtlinien des Flugs und Schalls, und dann verwandeln sich die Räume wieder und spiegeln eine selbstständige, neue audiovisuelle Sprache.

Der Bezug zum Theater der Erinnerung in der poetischen Beschreibung der Künstlerin scheint kein Zufall zu sein. Obwohl dieses Theater des 16. Jahrhunderts lediglich durch einen fragmentarischen Text erhalten geblieben ist, regt es noch immer die Fantasie in dem Wunsch an, ein ultimatives Schema der Erinnerung zu schaffen. Es gilt als faszinierender, bahnbrechender Versuch, das Netzwerk der Erinnerung durch die Verbindung von Räumlichem und Performativem darzustellen: Der Raum ist stufenförmig aufgebaut (wie ein Amphitheater), wobei diese Abstufung eine hierarchische und kategorische Bedeutung hat. Mythologische Figuren stehen auf den Stufen und reaktivieren ein komplexes Netzwerk von Affinitäten und internen Beziehungen.

Hes Yassours Anspielung auf das Theater der Erinnerung ist bedeutsam, da die Sprache, die sie im Lauf der Jahre in ihren Installationen entwickelt hat, in zweierlei Hinsicht einzigartig und innovativ ist: in der räumlichen und performativen Dimension. Mit diesen erkundet sie Raumstrukturen, die ein Muster von Beziehungen, Erinnerung und Vergessen projizieren und in denen auch ein Ausdruck der Gegenwart enthalten ist. Das Räumliche und das Performative weben das vielschichtige Netzwerk von Kontexten und Ausdrücken in jeder Ausstellung neu zusammen.

Für die Ausstellung in Recklinghausen, die Klang und Projektionen beinhaltet, schuf die Künstlerin vier Rauminstallationen, von denen jede teils Forschungslabor, teils Sammlungsraum oder auch eine Theaterbühne zu sein scheint. Es ist ein Geflecht aus Materialstücken, bildlichen Erinnerungen, einem Widerhall der Gegenwart und Elementen der Disziplinen, in denen sie als Künstlerin und Forscherin arbeitete.

Hes Yassour erwähnt in ihrer Beschreibung, dass das Theater der Erinnerung tiefgründig-reflektierend in ihrer künstlerischen Arbeit nachklingt. Reflektierende Kunst sucht nach dem Wesentlichen der Kunstproduktion und verortet die Kunst als Sprache und ihre Wirkungsweise als eine Umwandlung. Hes Yassour spielt in fast allen Bildern und Kontexten auf reflexive Elemente an – etwa eine kognitive Landkarte oder ein Museum, das sowohl Gehirn als auch Verstand ist; und in der von ihr erwähnten Installation entwickelt sie, angeregt vom Fledermaus-Forschungslabor, eine eigenständige, audiovisuelle Sprache.

Wie oben erwähnt stellt die kognitive Landkarte ein wesentliches Element ihres Werks dar. Ausschlaggebend war, dass sie als Studentin in „Echtzeit“ mit dem aufkommenden, reichen Diskurs der Umweltgeografie vertraut wurde, während

This is significant to the discussion at hand, since for fifty years the environmental perception of geography has been dealing with questions of spatial relationships and orientations,[4] as well as the role of the sensory experience of sound in spatial memory.[5]

Hes Yassour's encounter with the Weizmann Institute of Science researchers touches, through the prism of her art, upon a fascinating intersection of three parallel disciplines—science, contemporary art, and environmental geography. In the specific context of her work, it is linked to her early research of the mental map and her long-term work over the years in spatial perception. The researchers in the bat laboratory concentrated on issues of spatial cognition, navigation, spatial memory, and social memory. Their research provided neural-based evidence for a "cognitive map," in the wild, to a distance of a hundred kilometers in bats. The evidence may also suggest that the bats have social-spatial cognition.

The research labs offered Hes Yassour additional perspectives for exploring the spatial and the temporal. In her Recklinghausen exhibition, she embedded spatiality with a significant emphasis on the perception of time.

One should physically experience the sense of temporality in each of the four installations that include projections reflecting through the items on display and through space. Time in these installations echoes a "long duration," embedded in each installation in a different way, a different relation to space. Both the "naturalia" and the "artificilia," both time and space, are intertwined in her work like networks or webbing undergoing a slow process of covering, exposing, and elimination. In landscapes that may or may not be desolate, watchtowers rise up like theater figures or ghosts moving through the landscape, or like the masts of ships that lost their way, and a deceptively pastoral landscape gives substance to feelings of violence and anxiety.

The deep currents of the entirety of her work described in this essay is as if it had been immersed into the *Eroded Landscapes* installation with a new, powerful expression charged with present time.

It depicts an audio-visual, spatial, and performative landscape-like vision. A handful of figures, in black, stride as if on a tiered theater stage, not horizontal like in a theatre of an eternal memory but rather the inclined stage, a theatre of emergency. Secure in the routine, the figures move over a steep slope, thin as a fragile layer of ice, unaware of the abyss and the parallel reality below. The surface unfolding before us becomes a thin membrane that appears to cover the retina. In the front surface, close-up and sensual, sandy soil imported from elsewhere pours from the maw of massive devices.

The sound, composed by Jonathan Berger, charges the film with a sense of urgency. The sound of a hand writing profusely on a piece of paper, as if it were aware of time running out. A continuous muffled echo of an approaching storm, transforming the internal storm, increases the pressure of the hand on the paper and the drawing tempo, like a quick breath

sie bereits als Künstlerin arbeitete. Die zeitgenössische Kunst übernahm und subsumierte den räumlichen und später den performativen Wandel ebenfalls (so Vito Acconci und Robert Morris). Aber obwohl die bahnbrechende Philosophie an diesem Wendepunkt in beiden Bereichen vor allem der Phänomenalismus Maurice Merleau-Pontys war, entwickelte jeder einen eigenen Diskurs. Hes Yassour arbeitete in beiden. Das ist für die vorliegende Argumentation wichtig, denn die Umweltwahrnehmung der Geografie beschäftigt sich seit fünfzig Jahren mit Fragen der räumlichen Beziehungen und Orientierungen[4] und auch damit, welche Rolle das Klangerlebnis für die räumliche Erinnerung hat.[5]

Hes Yassours Begegnung mit den Forschern des Weizmann Institute of Science berührt über das Prisma ihrer Kunst eine faszinierende Schnittstelle dreier paralleler Disziplinen: der Wissenschaft, der zeitgenössischen Kunst und der Umweltgeografie. Im Kontext ihres Werks bedeutet das die Verbindung ihrer frühen Erforschung der kognitiven Landkarte und ihrer jahrelangen Beschäftigung mit der räumlichen Wahrnehmung. Die Wissenschaftler im Fledermauslabor konzentrierten sich auf Fragen der Raumkognition, Navigation, räumlichen Erinnerung und des sozialen Gedächtnisses. Ihre Forschungsarbeit erbrachte neural-basierte Beweise für eine „kognitive Karte" im Maßstab von hundert Kilometern bei Fledermäusen in freier Wildbahn. Der Nachweis kann auch darauf hindeuten, dass Fledermäuse eine sozialräumliche Wahrnehmung haben.

Das Labor lieferte Hes Yassour zusätzliche Anhaltspunkte für die Analyse der Raum- und Zeitwahrnehmung. In der Ausstellung in Recklinghausen verband sie die Räumlichkeit mit einer klaren Betonung der Zeitwahrnehmung. Der Betrachter sollte in allen vier Installationen die Zeitlichkeit körperlich fühlen, die durch Projektionen, Ausstellungsstücke und den Raum reflektiert wird. Zeit bedeutet in diesen Installationen eine „lange Dauer" und steht in jeder einzelnen in einer anderen Beziehung zum Raum. Sowohl die „Naturalien" als auch die „Artefakte", Zeit und Raum, sind in Penny Hes Yassours Werk wie Netze oder Gewebe verflochten und durchlaufen einen langsamen Prozess des Abdeckens, Freilegens und der Beseitigung. In Landschaften, die trostlos sein können oder auch nicht, ragen Wachtürme auf, die sich wie Theaterfiguren oder Geister durch die Landschaft bewegen oder wie Masten verirrter Schiffe; eine täuschend pastorale Landschaft lässt Gefühle von Gewalt und Angst aufkommen.

Es ist, als ob die eindringliche Tiefe ihres hier vorgestellten Œuvres in die Installation *Eroded Landscapes* übergegangen sei und sie mit einem neuen, kraftvollen Ausdruck der Gegenwart aufgeladen habe. Dargestellt ist eine audiovisuelle, räumliche und performative landschaftsartige Vision. Eine Handvoll schwarze Figuren schreiten voran, als würden sie sich auf einer gestuften Theaterbühne befinden. Diese Bühne ist nicht horizontal wie im Theater der ewigen Erinnerung, sondern geneigt, ein „Theater des Notfalls". Mit routinierter Sicherheit bewegen sich die Figuren über einen steilen Hang

heightened by a quick pulse. Four screens display different sequences, like layers of the same mental map shape-shifting in space: “Invisible and visible continual movements, streams of water, winds, sand, hostility, aggression, arbitrariness of the heart, grand plans, loaded boundaries, physical and mental, prejudices, fears, abandonments.”[6]

1 Meir Agassi, “Sculpture as a Mental Map,” *Studio* 30 (February 1992), pp. 44–45.

2 Jean-François Chevrier, “Mental Fabrication,” in Penny Yassour, *Mental Maps – Production Halls, Mental Maps – Default Spaces,* exh. cat. (curator Galia Bar Or), Mishkan Museum of Art (Ein Harod, 1994), p. 40.

3 Echolalia, a symptom of uncontrollable repetition of words. *Penny Yassour: Echolalia*, ed. Bernhard Balkenhol, exh. cat. Kasseler Kunstverein, Fridericianum, Kassel 2000/01 (Marburg, 2001).

4 Rodney White, John Kirtland Wright, David Lowenthal, and Douglas Pocock, among others.

5 Douglas Pocock, “Sound and the Geographer,” *Geography* 74, no. 3 (June 1989), pp. 193–200.

6 From the artist’s sketchbook.

vorwärts, der dünn ist wie eine zerbrechliche Eisschicht, ohne den Abgrund oder die Parallelwelt darunter wahrzunehmen. Die Oberfläche, die sich vor unseren Augen entfaltet, wird zu einer dünnen Membran, welche die Netzhaut zu bedecken scheint. Im Vordergrund, ganz nah und sinnlich, gießen die Schlünde massiger Geräte von woanders importierten Sand aus. Der von Jonathan Berger komponierte Ton lädt den Film mit einem Gefühl der Dringlichkeit auf. Es ist das Geräusch zu hören, wie eine Hand eifrig auf ein Blatt Papier schreibt, als wäre sie sich bewusst, dass die Zeit drängt. Das kontinuierliche, gedämpfte Echo eines herannahenden Sturms, das den inneren Sturm umwandelt, steigert den von der Hand auf das Papier ausgeübten Druck und die Schreibgeschwindigkeit, wie schnelles Atmen durch den Pulsschlag beschleunigt wird. Vier Bildschirme zeigen verschiedene Sequenzen, Schichten derselben kognitiven Landkarte, die im Raum ihre Gestalt verändern: „Unsichtbare und sichtbare kontinuierliche Bewegungen, Wasserströme, Winde, Sand, Feindseligkeit, Aggression, Willkür des Herzens, große Pläne, physisch und mental beladene Grenzen, Vorurteile, Ängste, Verlassenheit."[6]

1 Siehe Agassi, Meir: „Sculpture as a Mental Map", in: *Studio,* 30, Februar 1992, S. 44/45.

2 Chevrier, Jean-François: „Mental Fabrication", in: *Penny Yassour. Mental Maps – Production Halls. Mental Maps – Default Spaces,* Ausst.-Kat. Mishkan Museum of Art (kuratiert von Galia Bar Or), Ein Harod 1994, S. 40.

3 Echolalie bezeichnet das stereotype, sinnlos erscheinende Nachsprechen von Worten oder Sätzen. – *Penny Yassour. Echolalia,* hrsg. von Bernhard Balkenhol, Ausst.-Kat. Kasseler Kunstverein, Fridericianum, Kassel 2000/01, Marburg 2001.

4 Rodney White, John Kirtland Wright, David Lowenthal, Douglas Pocock und andere.

5 Siehe Pocock, Douglas: „Sound and the Geographer", in: *Geography,* Bd. 74, Nr. 3, Juni 1989, S. 193–200.

6 Aus dem Skizzenbuch der Künstlerin.

RESONANCE TOWERS – BETWEEN MEMORY AND OBLIVION

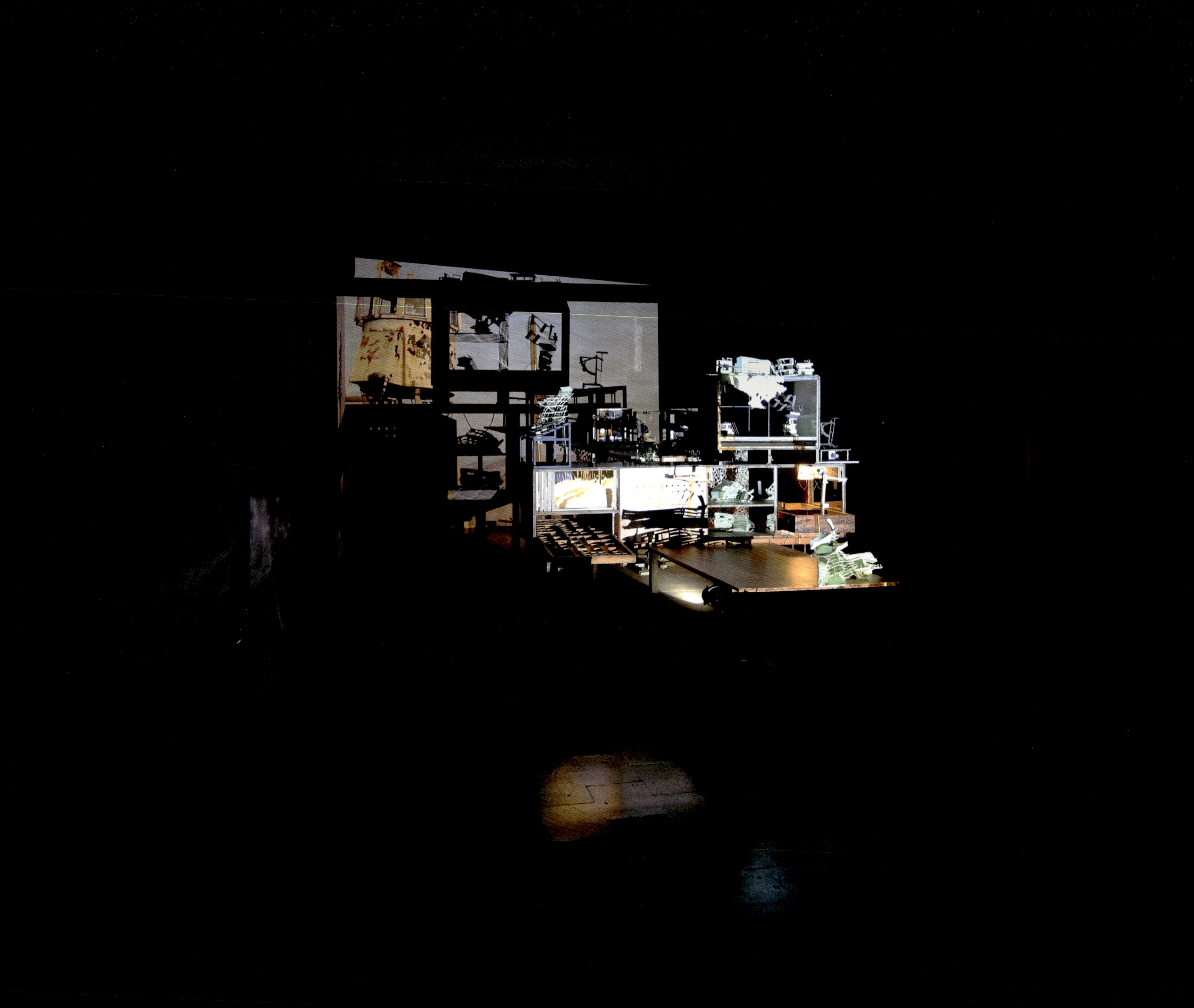

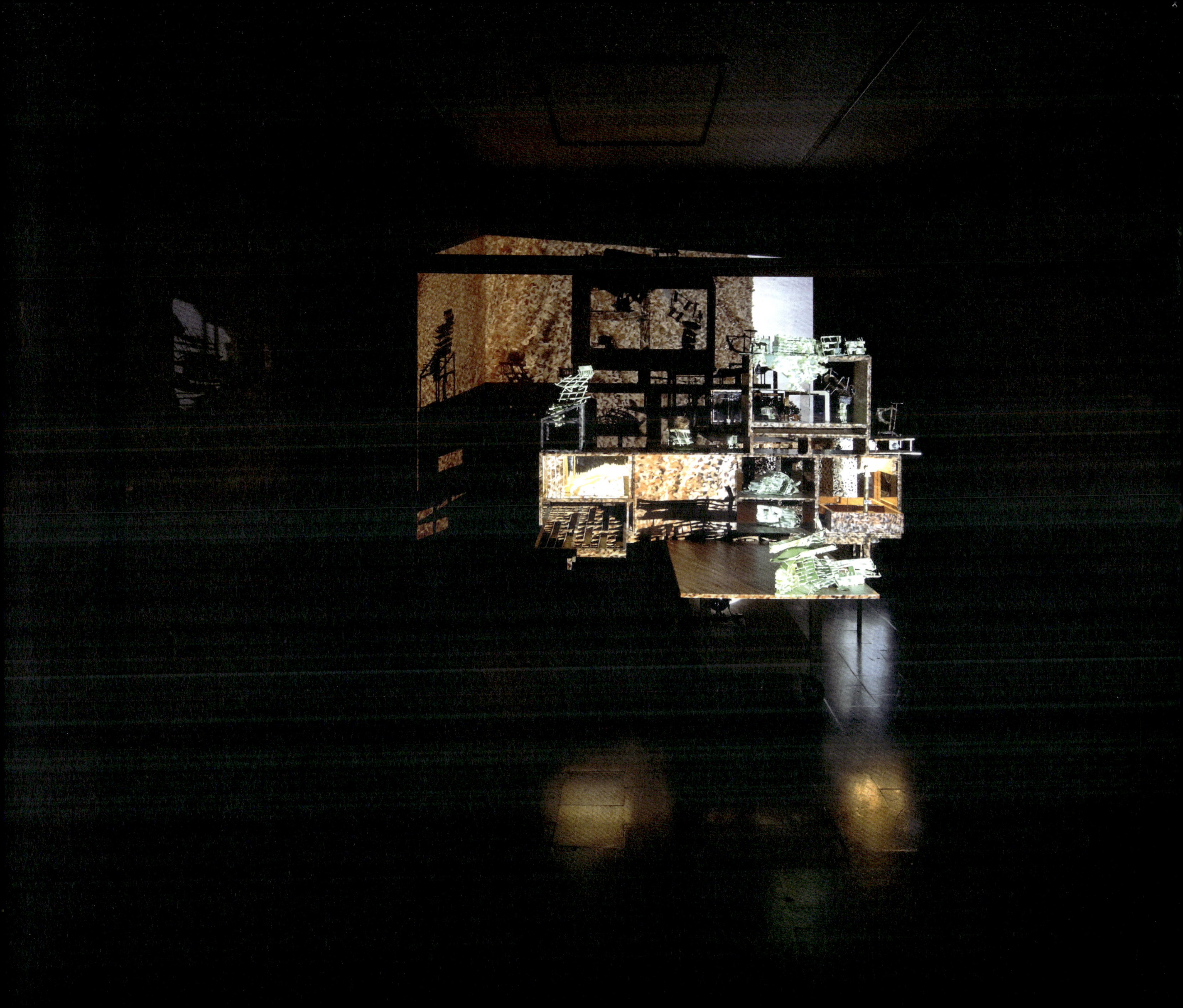

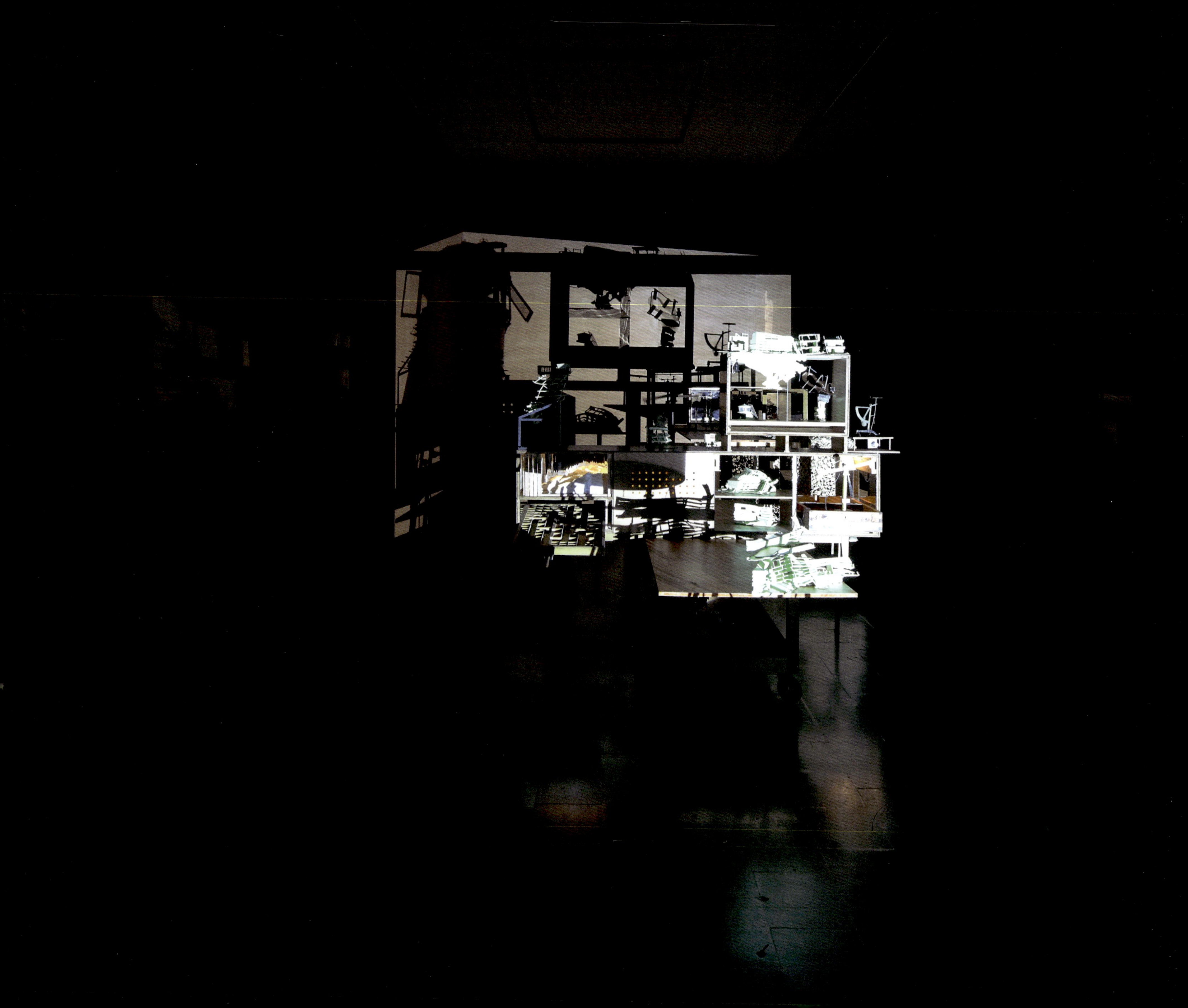

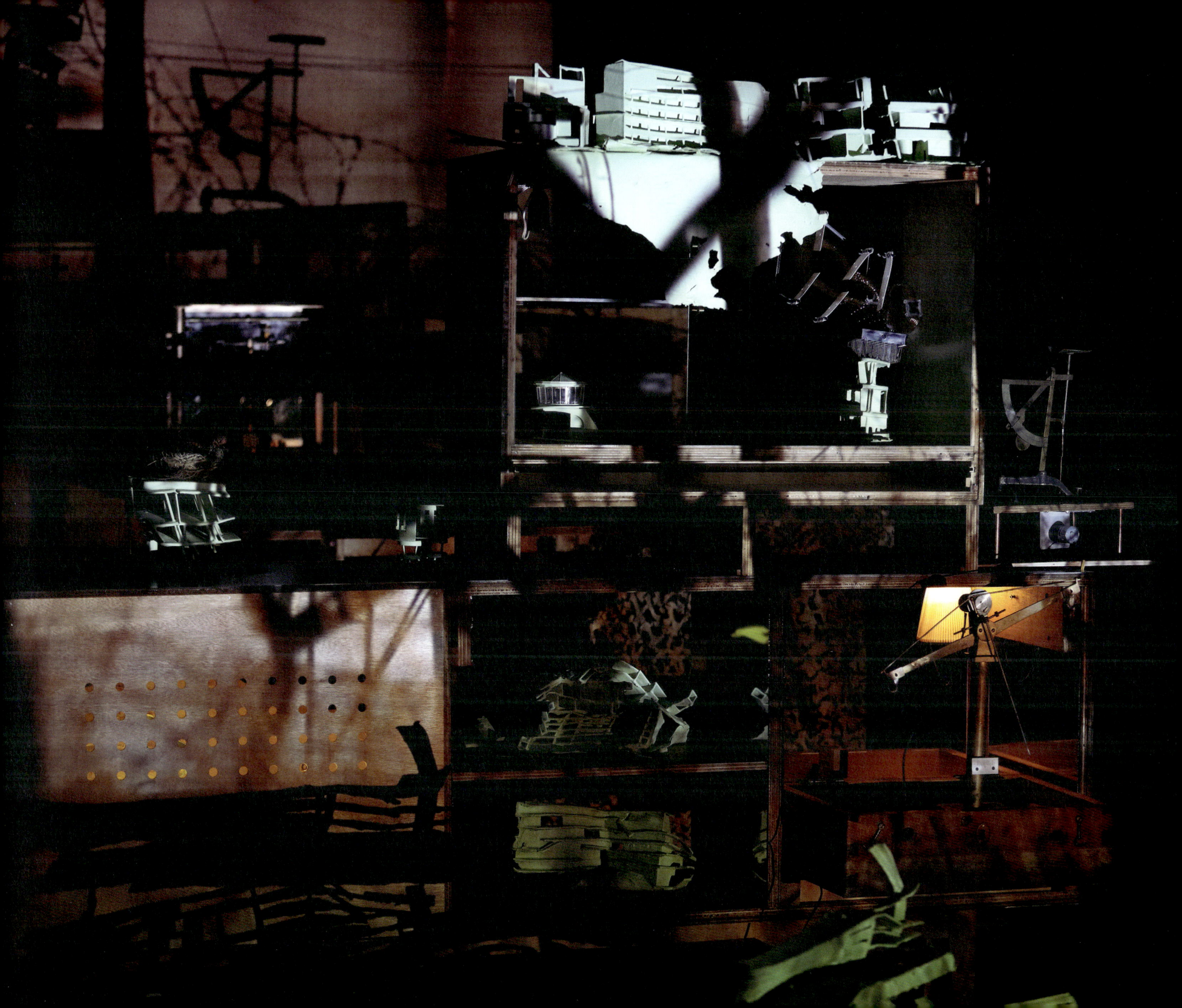

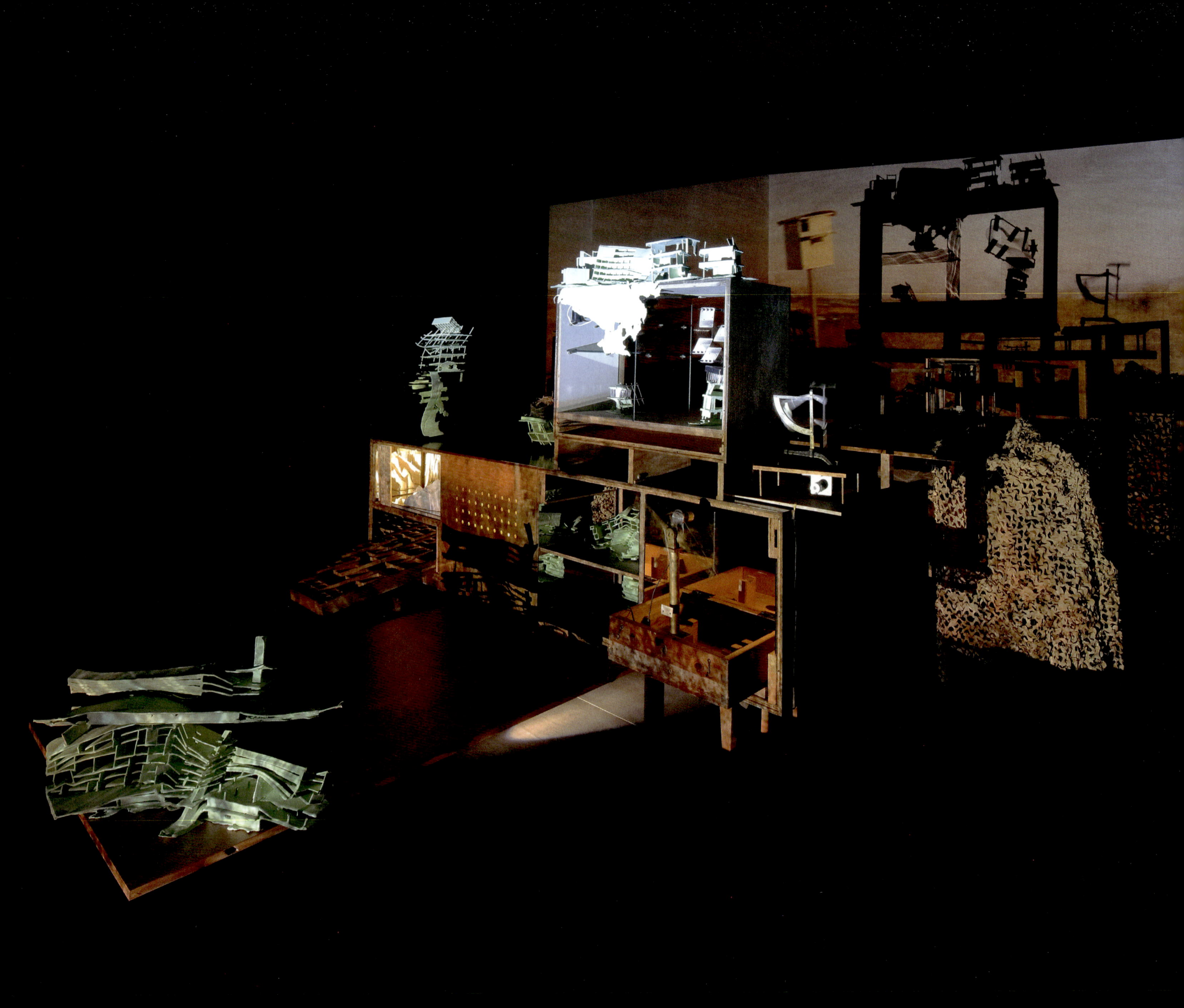

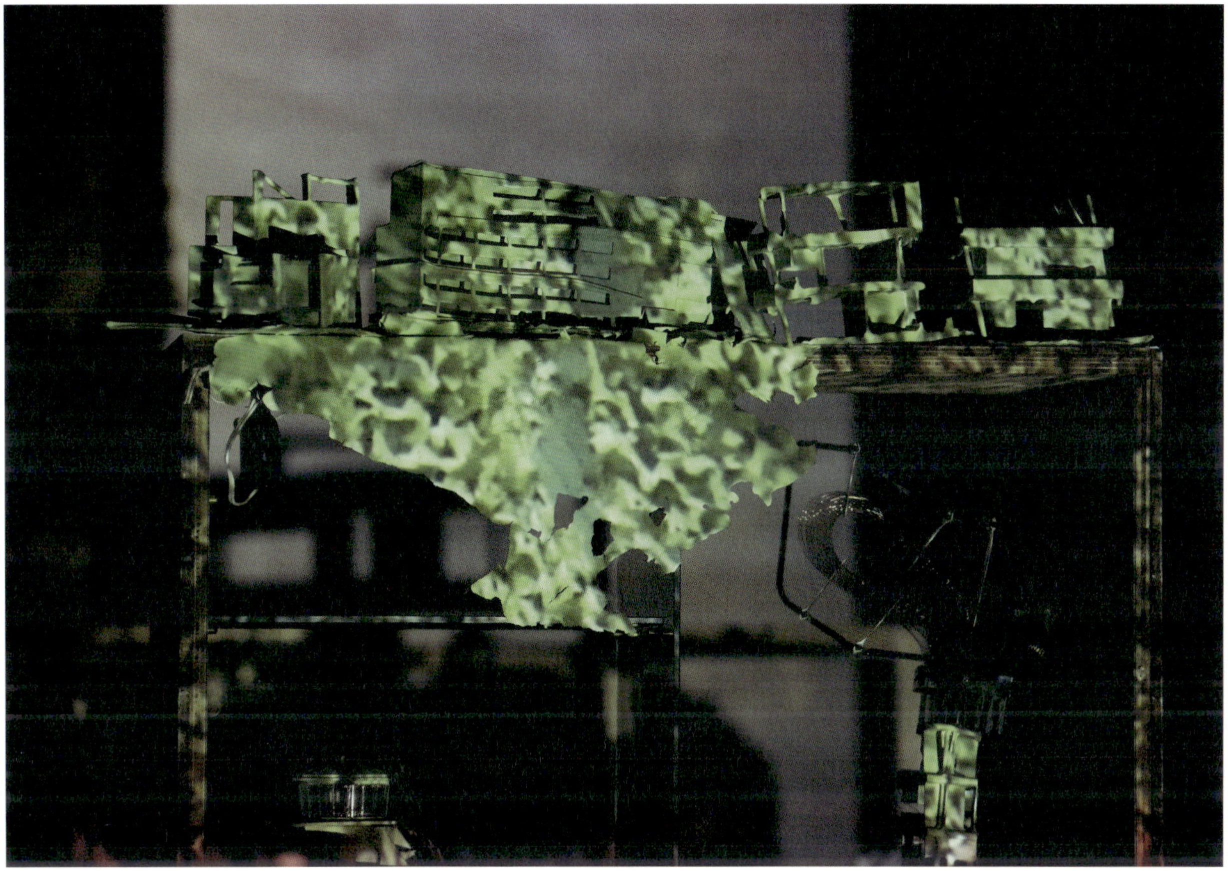

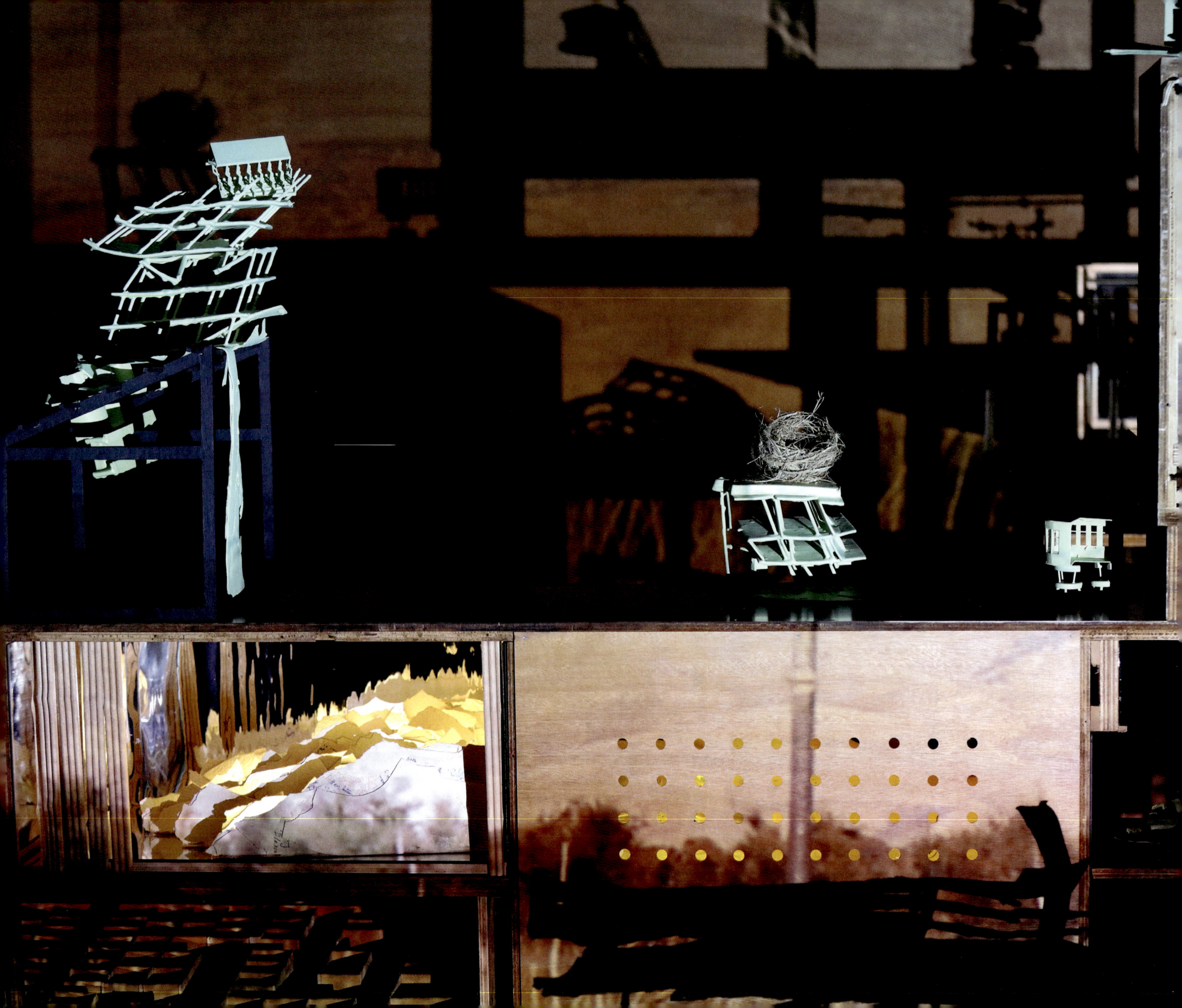

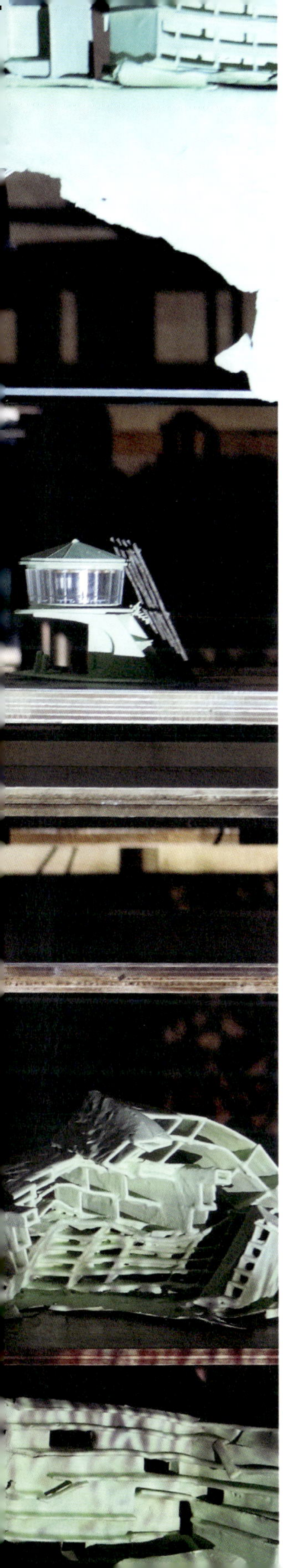

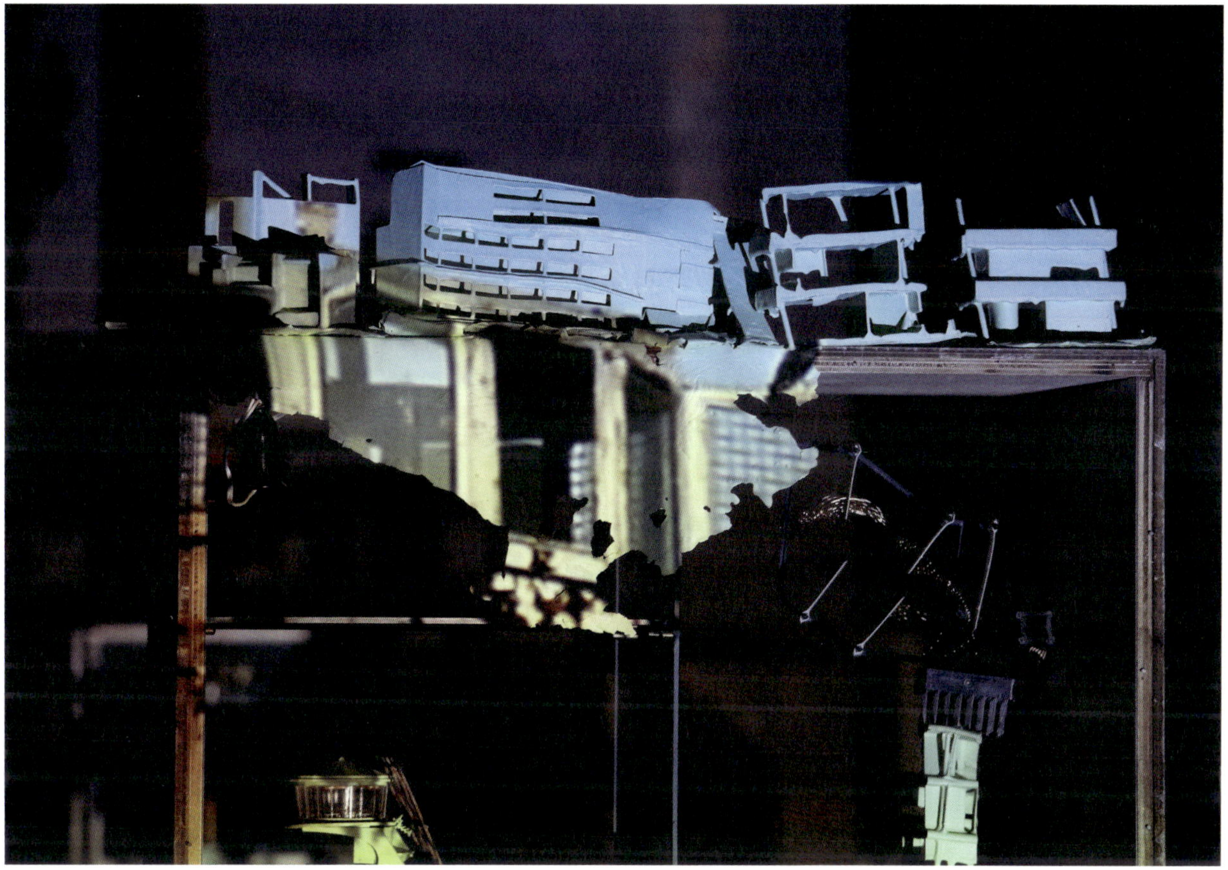

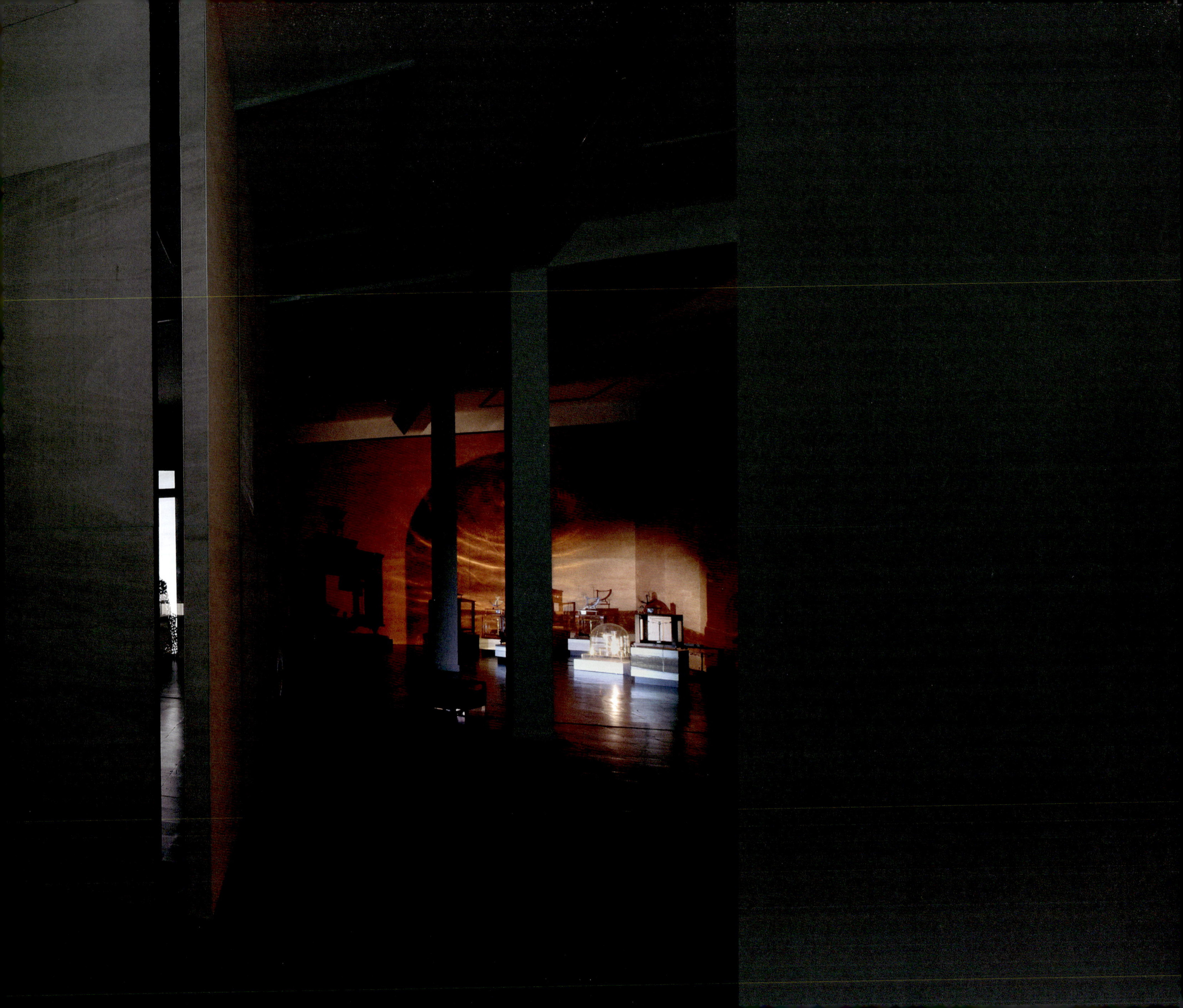

A·BAN·DON·MENT

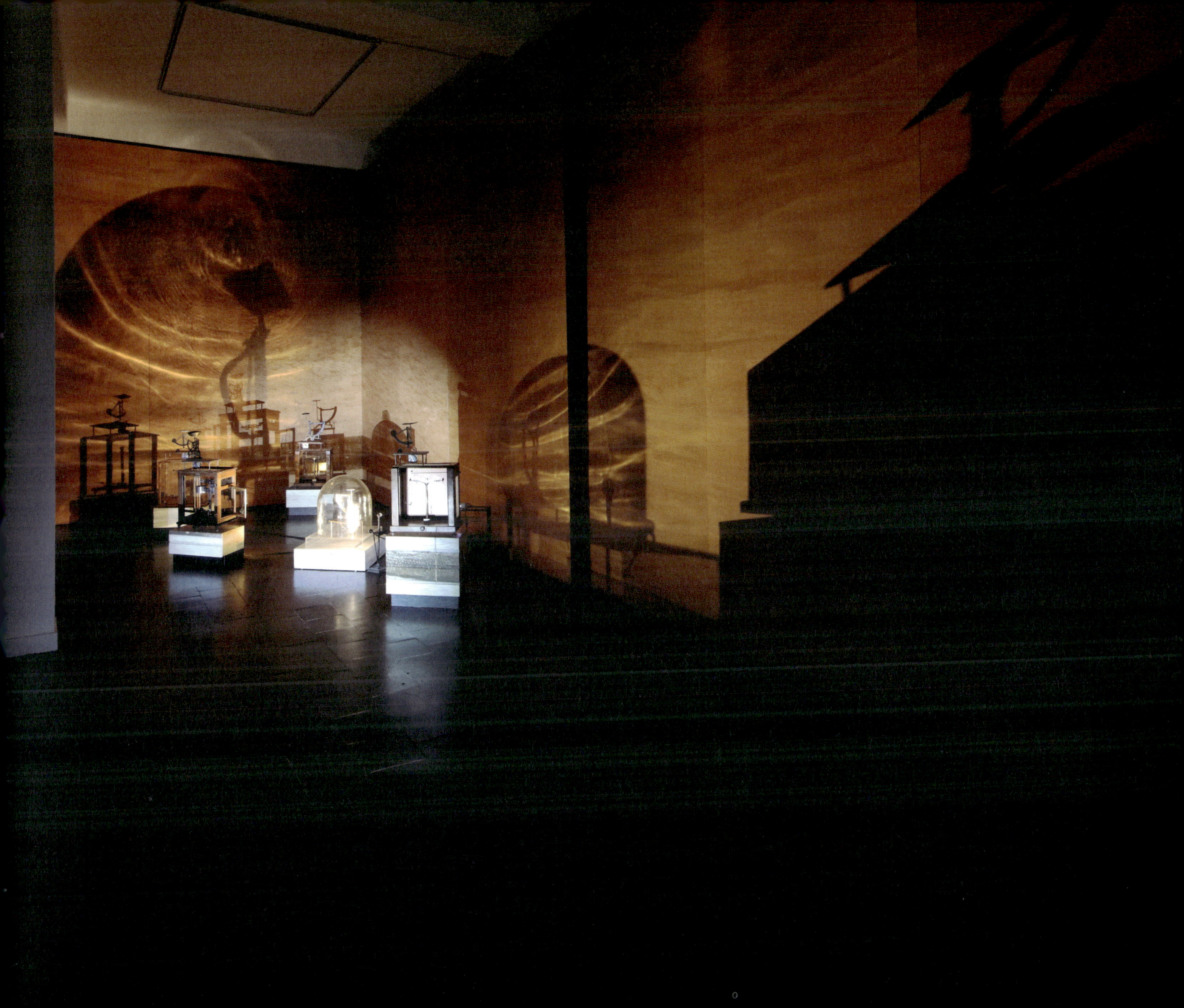

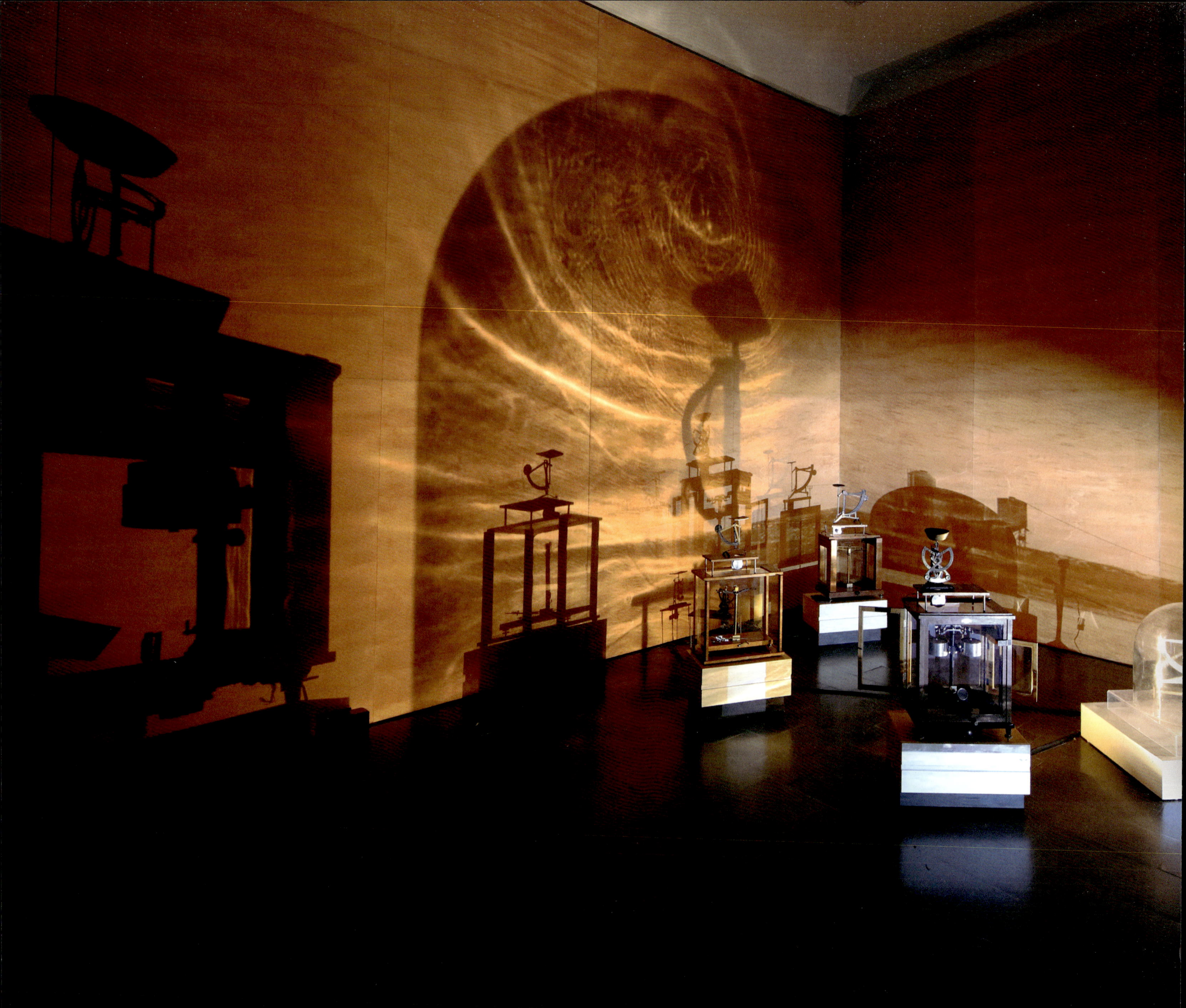

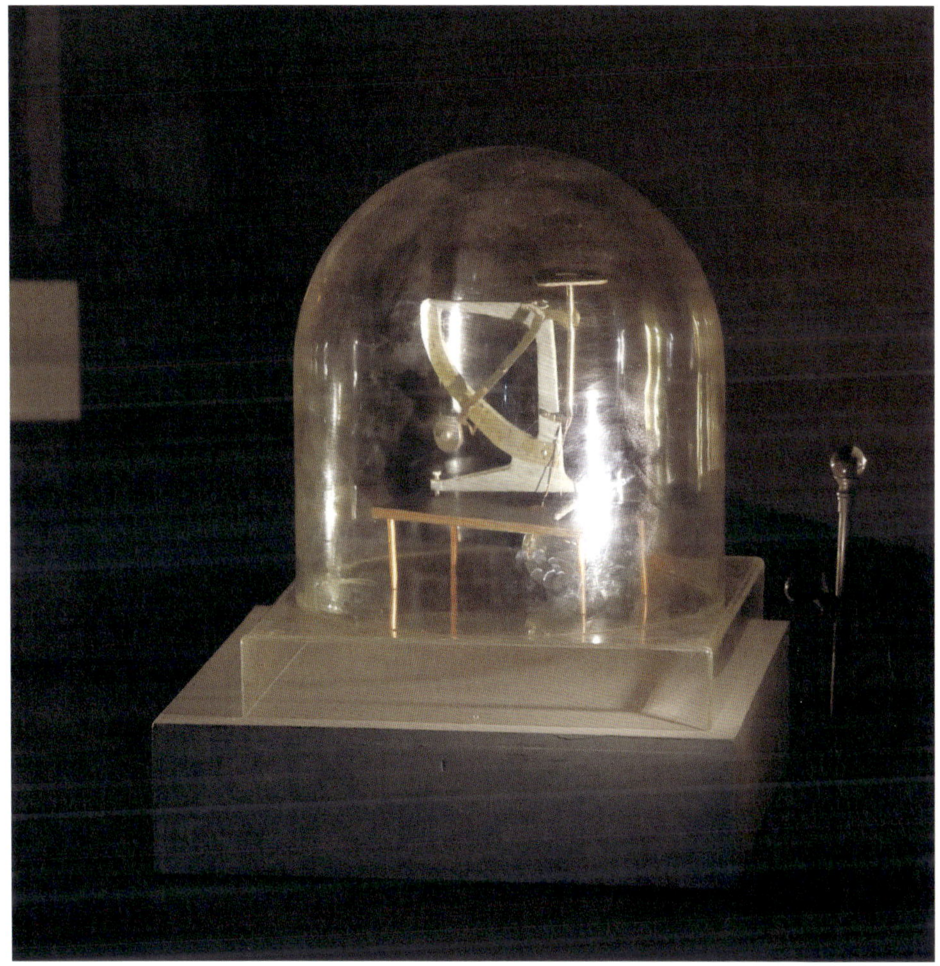

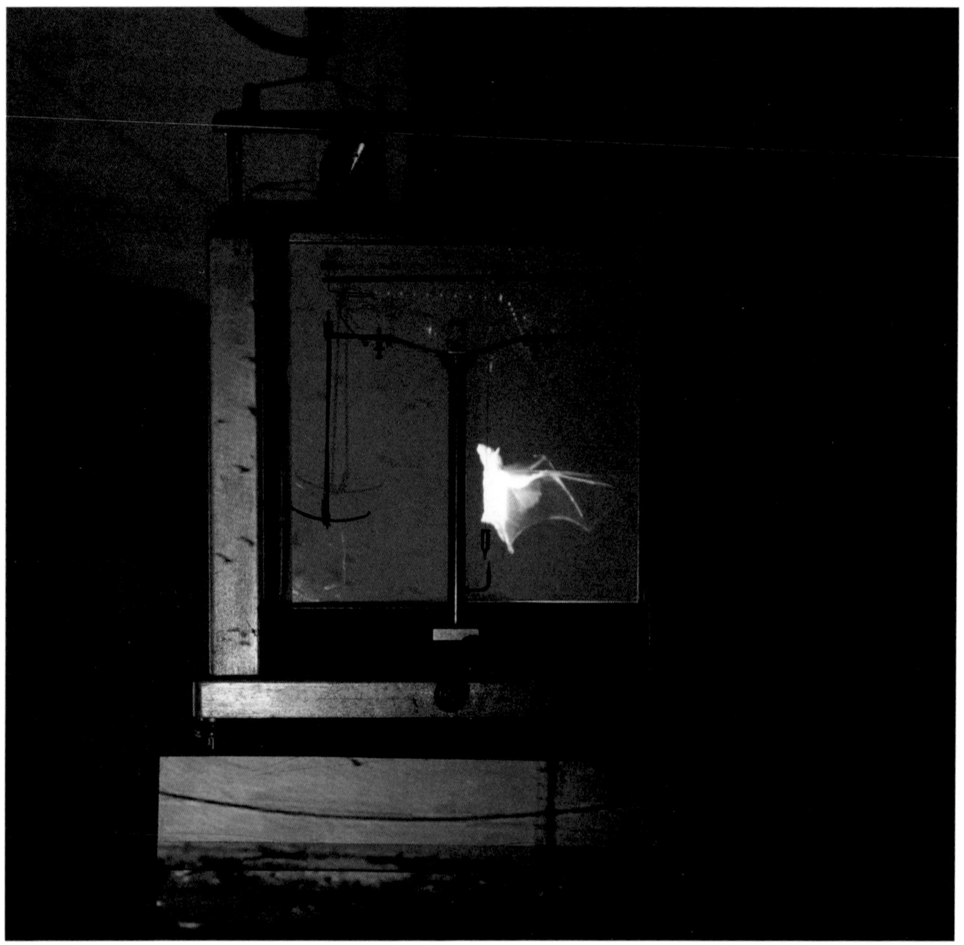

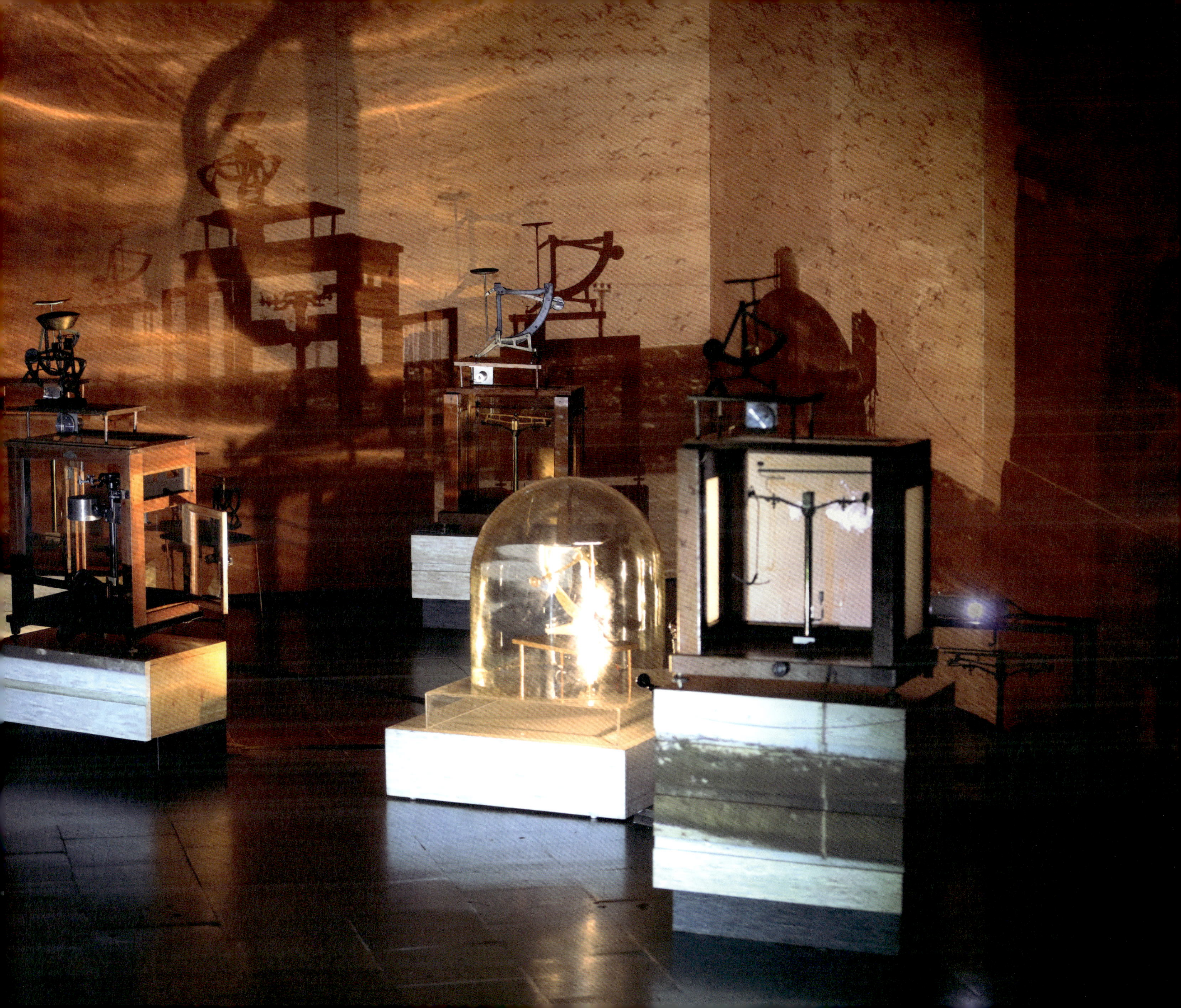

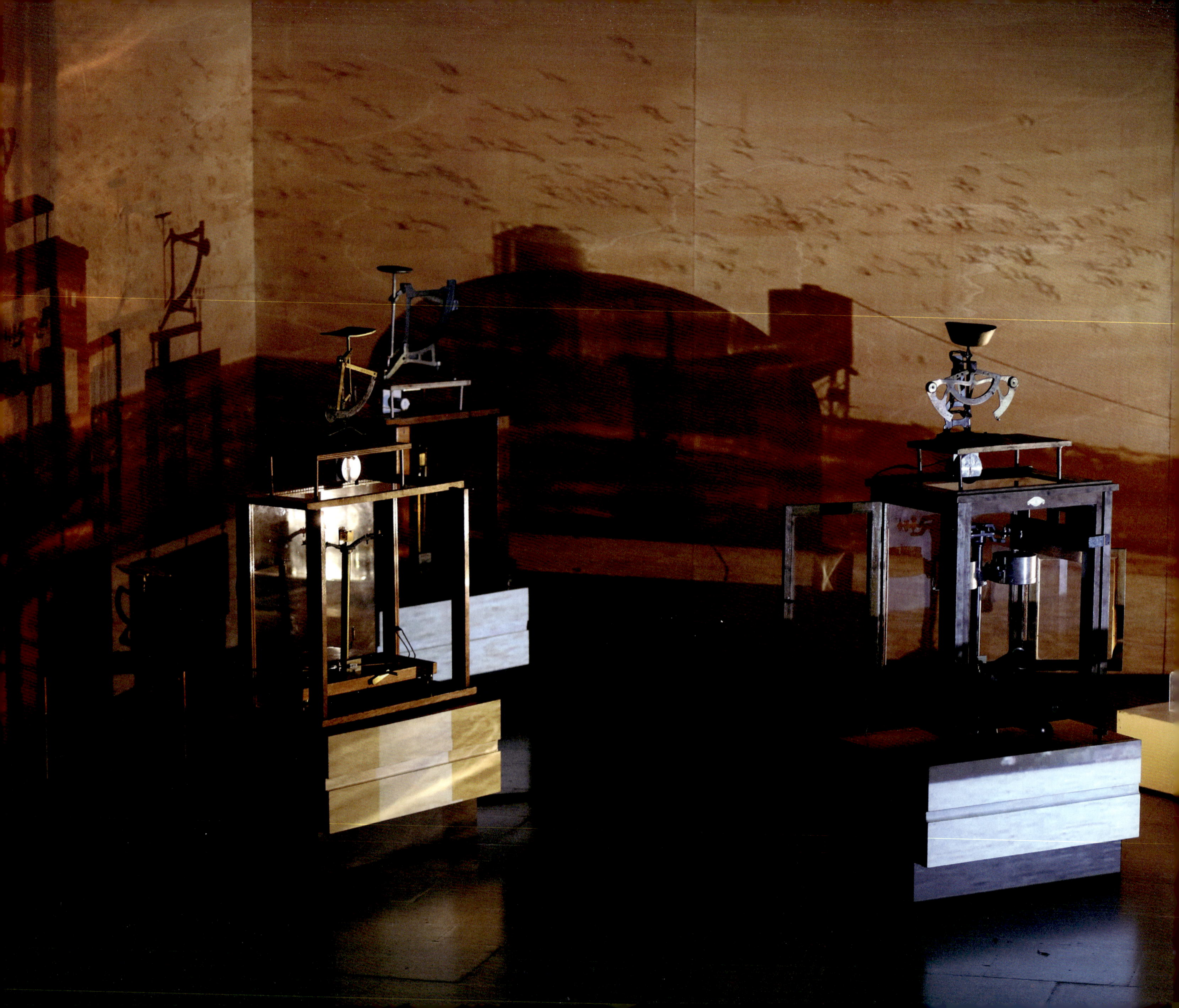

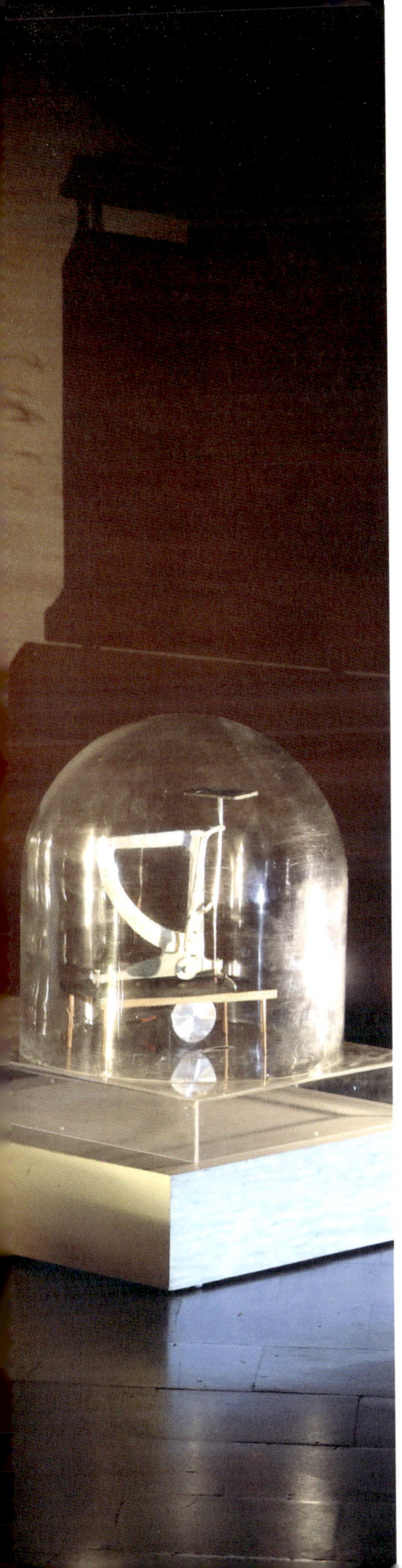

DEVASTATION IN A MINOR KEY

NIMROD REITMAN

"Corresponding to these phantasmagorias of the market, where people appear only as types, are the phantasmagorias of the interior, which are constituted by man's imperious need to leave the imprint of his private individual existence on the rooms he inhabits." WALTER BENJAMIN, *Arcades Project*[1]

Walter Benjamin's *Arcades Project,* a perpetually incomplete draft of a grand cartography of an unmapped nineteenth century, was modeled on the enchantment engaging the inability to see. Rather than directing one's vision into an "objective reality," Benjamin insisted on a logic vacillating between the spectral and the dead. For Benjamin, this logic, which stems from a blinding fascination caused by capitalist fetishism, is an inherent element of Modernity.[2] One of the central concepts upon which Benjamin based his wanderings into the Parisian arcade—for in Benjamin's case arcades may well have the same allegorical emblematics of death as in both of Nicolas Poussin's pastorals *Et in arcadia ego*—is phantasmagoria, in other words, what resists a recognizable catalogue of political, poetical, perceptual determinations, and instead registers a sense of disruption and electric disturbance premised in visual dissidence and furtive gestural experience. Irrationality imbibed with image projections, music, mirrors, smoke, shadow puppetry, and other theatrical devices, phantasmagoria elides its own poetic powers. The demand, it seems, is to look inwards and to look for the dead that any phantasma habitually contains, even as its dream logic fades and obscures logical decoding. The violence implicitly carried by Benjamin's *Arcades* demarcates an attempt to awaken utopian possibilities and exorcise the nightmare of the real, only in order to barter it for a more devastating grid of utterance, leaving one to choose between the bad and the worse. Penny Hes Yassour's *Resonance*

VERWÜSTUNG IN MOLL

NIMROD REITMAN

„Den spezifischen Phantasmagorien des Marktes, in denen der Mensch nur noch als Typus auftritt, entsprechen die des Interieurs, das durch dessen Bedürfnis konstituiert wird, im Wohnraum die Spur seiner Privatexistenz aufzudrücken."
WALTER BENJAMIN, *Das Passagen-Werk*[1]

Walter Benjamins *Passagen-Werk,* der unvollendet gebliebene Entwurf einer grandiosen Kartografie für das unvermessene 19. Jahrhundert, setzt jenen Zauber voraus, der die Unfähigkeit zu sehen bewirkt. Statt den Blick auf eine „objektive Wirklichkeit" zu richten, bestand Benjamin auf einer Logik, die zwischen dem Geisterhaften und dem Toten schwankt. Für ihn ist diese Logik, die von der blendenden Faszinationskraft des Warenfetischismus herrührt, ein inhärentes Element der Moderne.[2] Eine der zentralen Ideen, auf denen er seine Streifzüge durch die Pariser Ladenpassagen aufbaute (im Fall Benjamins mögen die Passagen durchaus für die gleiche allegorische Todesemblematik stehen wie Nicolas Poussins beide pastorale Gemälde *Die Hirten von Arkadien*), ist die Phantasmagorie, oder anders gesagt das, was sich der erkennbaren Einordnung nach politischen, poetischen und wahrnehmungsbasierten Kriterien entzieht und stattdessen ein Gefühl von Zerrissenheit und elektrisierender Unruhe zum Ausdruck bringt, das auf visueller Unstimmigkeit und verstohlenen Gesten basiert. Auf absurde Weise durchtränkt von Bildprojektionen, Musik, Spiegeln, Rauch, Schattenspiel und anderen theatralischen Mitteln, entlässt die Phantasmagorie ihre eigenen poetischen Kräfte. Es scheint, als bestehe die Forderung darin, nach innen zu blicken und nach dem Toten zu suchen, das jedem Phantasma für gewöhnlich innewohnt – sogar, wenn die Traumlogik verblasst und dadurch eine Deutung nach logischen Kriterien erschwert wird.

Towers – between Memory and Oblivion follows such a Benjaminian logic, mobilizing the architectural model and its many configurations in order to denote spaces that are not present and whose non-presence still relentlessly manifests its spectral spatially. One could argue that the model is *par excellence* the vehicle designed to designate that which is not yet there and yet promises to arrive. But Hes Yassour's resonating towers lend themselves to a realm of dreamscapes where logic no longer abides the spectator either to memory or futurity. Unlike the architectural model, which gazes forward toward the unbuilt yet with a potential to be built, Hes Yassour's models capture spaces that were always already and never destined to be realized; an assemblage of *objet trouvé*, a graveyard of architectural dreams reanimated through cinema.

An amalgamation of architectures as armatures—fortifications abutted to security structures and other urban apparatuses of ambiguous function—*Resonance Towers* confronts us with a surveillance state gone mad, its digestive system turned inside out to reveal a landscape of cannibalized, building-like things, forged together to create something larger than the sum of its parts. Moving around the installation unfolds a catalogue of cinematic syntagms, casting a foreboding effect that intensifies as the work accumulates, even as distinct borders between the real and phantasy are blurred into a porous veil which summons the appearance of the familiar now revealed to be the most defamiliarizing.

Any attempt to explain the deepening sense of menace of *Resonance Towers* falls short of iconographic sorting. Analyzing each component in isolation—the pendulums, the projection lights, the models, the enclosures, the polymer nets, the soundtrack—cannot account for the claustrophobic, yet at the same time, ravishing and rich effect of the work. Violence, as we have learned from Walter Benjamin, Hannah Arendt, and Giorgio Agamben, always tends to have an unremarkable manifestation when viewed in close-up. It is precisely the banal or everyday-ness of Hes Yassour's objects, amassed into a Frankensteinian machine, that gives a caustic realization of how violence operates. It is through the inassimilable abyss between the object and its effect that violence metabolizes itself through political and aesthetical networks. Philosophically speaking, and philosophy spanning Plato to Martin Heidegger has always been in a ready position to participate in oppressive regiments, one could conceive of the work's effect in terms of Immanuel Kant's mathematical sublime, namely of the anxiety provoked by the violence of the unquantifiable. (In a different point and time, Rainer Maria Rilke would have said, "Beauty is the beginning of terror.")[3] Artists as varied as William Kentridge, Aziz + Cutcher, and Anri Sala have tended to such Kantian definitions of the sublime verging on the unpresentable, as they offered their own version of polyphonic phantasmagoria. For this kind of art form, close in its components to Richard Wagner's *Gesamtkunstwerk*, can augment the work's impact to horrific proportions. In many cases, the result is a masculinist display of bravura and skill, showing "too much process" in a genre that subtends the spectral; an over-explication of ideas in a too pronounced manner

Die implizite Gewalt in Benjamins *Passagen* stellt einen Versuch dar, utopische Möglichkeiten zu eröffnen und den Albtraum des Realen auszutreiben, nur um ihn gegen ein noch verheerenderes Ausdrucksraster einzutauschen, sodass lediglich die Wahl zwischen dem Schlechten und dem Schlimmeren bleibt. Penny Hes Yassours *Resonance Towers – between Memory and Oblivion* folgt dieser Benjamin'schen Logik und mobilisiert das Architekturmodell in seinen vielfältigen Gestaltungsformen, um Räume anzudeuten, die nicht vorhanden sind und deren Abwesenheit dennoch schonungslos ihre geisterhafte Räumlichkeit manifestiert. Es ließe sich argumentieren, dass das Modell das Vehikel par excellence ist, um das aufzuzeigen, was zwar noch nicht da ist, jedoch sein Eintreffen bereits verheißt. Aber Hes Yassours schwingende Türme bieten sich als Traumlandschaften an, in denen die Logik den Betrachter nicht mehr an Erinnerungen oder Zukunftsvorstellungen bindet. Anders als ein Architekturmodell, das zwar auf das Unerbaute, möglicherweise aber zukünftig Errichtete blickt, fangen Hes Yassours Modelle Räume ein, die zu keinem Zeitpunkt ihre Verwirklichung anstreben; sie sind eine Ansammlung von *objets trouvés,* ein Friedhof architektonischer Träume, der durch filmische Mittel wiederbelebt wird. Durch die Verschmelzung von Bauwerken zu Panzerungen – zu Befestigungsanlagen, die auf Sicherheitskonstruktionen und anderen urbanen Apparaturen unklarer Funktion beruhen – konfrontiert uns *Resonance Towers* mit einem aus den Fugen geratenen Überwachungsstaat, dessen Verdauungssystem von innen nach außen gekehrt wurde und eine Landschaft mit ausgeschlachteten, gebäudeähnlichen Objekten offenbart, die zusammengeschmiedet wurden, um etwas entstehen zu lassen, das größer ist als die Summe seiner Teile. Betrachtet man die Installation von allen Seiten, entfaltet sich ein Katalog kinematischer Syntagmen; sie erwecken eine Vorahnung, die mit der Aufhäufung des Werks immer stärker wird, auch wenn die Grenzen zwischen Realität und Fantasie immer mehr zu einem porösen Schleier verschwimmen, der nun das eigentlich Vertraute als das Allerbefremdlichste entlarvt.

Jeder Versuch, das intensive Gefühl der Bedrohung zu erklären, das sich bei der Betrachtung der *Resonance Towers* einstellt, fällt hinter die ikonografische Sortierung zurück. Die isolierte Analyse der einzelnen Bestandteile – Pendel, Projektionslichter, Modelle, Umfriedungen, Kunststoffnetze und Klänge – kann die klaustrophobische und gleichzeitig hinreißend prachtvolle Wirkung der Türme nicht erklären. Wie wir von Walter Benjamin, Hannah Arendt und Giorgio Agamben gelernt haben, neigt Gewalt stets dazu, sich aus der Nähe betrachtet eher als unspektakulär darzustellen. Und gerade die Banalität oder Alltäglichkeit der Objekte Hes Yassours lässt sie in ihrer Anhäufung zu einer Frankensteinmaschine werden, die in aller Schärfe darlegt, wie Gewalt funktioniert. Durch die unüberbrückbare Kluft zwischen Gegenstand und Wirkung entsteht die Gewalt mithilfe politischer und ästhetischer Netzwerke. Aus philosophischer Sicht – und von Platon bis hin zu Martin Heidegger stand die Philosophie stets bereit, an unterdrückerischen Herrschaftsformen

that denies the dead their place and distances us from any relation to the phantastic. For the technology of phantasy is close but not identical to the way allegory operates textually, namely, tied to loose ends and affined to death, resisting any sort of recuperation or any sense of transcendence. Here, Hes Yassour offers a more lyrical version, almost in a minor key. In drawing attention to its title and the seeming space between memory and oblivion—of what no one really knows—*Resonance Towers* signal two poles that can no longer carry any signifiable denotations to the extent that memory and oblivion no longer behave as mere opposites. These attributes imply that substantial entities or objects or even perceptual processes, can stand up to one another, be given over to memory or oblivion, and even possibly mirror or refute each other, as they no longer behave as mere opposites. These attributes imply that substantial entities or objects or even perceptual processes, hold their own critical ground. However under the sway of the work's resonance—acoustic and optic—these phenomena can no longer stabilize into a recognizable entity. It could even be that Hes Yassour's installation hinges on this set of seemingly duplicitous pair that must collapse on itself, opting for the liminal space of the *between*.

A hybrid of filmic and architectural space confronts us in Hes Yassour's *a·ban·don·ment*. An ephemeral architecture made from projected images on the installation's plywood walls, the space of the gallery is duplicated through the animation of the model, which at the same time breaks away from its materiality. There is a sense of eroded sensation, where disruption becomes the law for deciphering what should otherwise remain illegible. The viewer is stupefied by the decadent vision, for the work is visually sumptuous and engrossing, inviting one to revel in its seeming unreadability. Like Sigmund Freud's mute death drive, the soundscape is kept in relative stillness, creating a tensional suspension for a musical resolution that fails to arrive.[4] The clash between the acoustic silence and the visual saturation creates a zone where identity remains perpetually undetermined, producing something that behaves like an alternative vision, perhaps in an overdetermined way.

On the right side of the installation, encased in a wood and glass cabinet, on its own, indeed abandoned, is a holographic image of a creature whose morphology remains ambiguous, spliced between a bat and a white bird. Taking its cues from Benjamin's angel of history, looking at the accumulating wreckage of historical ruins that he had identified with "progress," the bird-bat ostensibly spreads its wings, looking at the other side of the ever-menacing installation and yet remaining separate from it.[5] At this point, the marginal creature may well constitute the core of the work (in the sense of Roland Barthes's *punctum*), the very center upon which the work stands, or rather collapses. For what this creature sees is an incalculable number of doppelgangers: Hes Yassour has saturated the plywood's crepuscular sky with a moving image of a swarm of birds circling the space aimlessly and yet charging it with an impossible and portentous Hitchcockian effect.

mitzuwirken – könnte man die Wirkung der Türme unter dem Aspekt von Immanuel Kants Mathematisch-Erhabenem betrachten, nämlich als die Angst, die von der Gewalt des Unquantifizierbaren hervorgerufen wird.[3] (Unter anderen Umständen und in einer anderen Zeit hätte Rainer Maria Rilke wohl gesagt: „Schönheit ist der Anfang des Schreckens.")

Ganz unterschiedliche Künstler wie William Kentridge, Aziz + Cucher oder Anri Sala waren den Kant'schen Definitionen des Erhabenen am Rande des Nicht-Darstellbaren zugetan, wenn sie ihre eigene polyfone Phantasmagorie darlegten. Diese Kunstform mit ihren Richard Wagners Gesamtkunstwerk ähnelnden Komponenten ist nämlich in der Lage, die Wirkung des Werks in erschreckendem Ausmaß zu verstärken. Häufig ist das Ergebnis eine maskuline Zurschaustellung von Bravour und Können, die zu viel von einem Genre preisgibt, das dem Geisterhaften gegenüberliegt; ein übertriebenes und überdeutliches Erklären von Ideen, das den Toten ihren Platz verweigert und uns von jeglichem Bezug zum Fantastischen entfremdet. Die Technik der Fantasie ist der textlichen Allegorie zwar ähnlich, jedoch nicht mit ihr deckungsgleich; sie hängt an unerledigten und toten Dingen, widersteht allen Formen der Entspannung und jedem Anflug von Transzendenz. Hes Yassour bietet eine lyrischere Version an, gewissermaßen in Moll.

Resonance Towers – between Memory and Oblivion zieht die Aufmerksamkeit auf seinen Titel und auf den vermeintlichen Raum zwischen Erinnerung und Vergessen – wovon, weiß niemand wirklich; die Türme signalisieren zwei Pole, die in dem Maße, in dem Erinnerung und Vergessen sich nicht länger wie ein bloßes Gegensatzpaar verhalten, keine signifikanten Bedeutungen mehr tragen können. Diese Attribute implizieren, dass substanzielle Entitäten oder Objekte, aber auch Wahrnehmungsprozesse einander standhalten und der Erinnerung oder dem Vergessen überlassen werden können, einander möglicherweise sogar spiegeln oder widerlegen, indem sie ihren eigenen kritischen Boden behaupten. Unter den widerhallenden Schwingungen des Werks – akustisch wie auch optisch – können diese Phänomene sich nicht länger zu einem erkennbaren Gebilde stabilisieren. Es mag sogar sein, dass Hes Yassours Installation von diesem scheinbar doppelzüngigen Paar abhängig ist, das in sich selbst zusammenstürzen muss und sich so für den Grenzbereich des „Dazwischen" entscheidet.

Mit einer Synthese aus filmischem und architektonischem Raum sehen wir uns in Hes Yassours *a·ban·don·ment* konfrontiert. Als flüchtige Konstruktion aus Bildern, die auf die Sperrholzwände der Installation projiziert werden, wird der Ausstellungsraum mittels einer Animation des Modells dupliziert, das sich zugleich von seiner Stofflichkeit löst. Man verspürt ein destruktives Gefühl, bei dem die Zerschlagung zum Gesetz der Entschlüsselung dessen wird, was sonst unleserlich bliebe. Die dekadente Vorstellung raubt dem Betrachter die Sinne, denn das visuell üppige und fesselnde Werk lädt dazu ein, in seiner vermeintlichen Undeutbarkeit zu schwelgen. Gemahnend an Sigmund Freuds stummen Todestrieb[4] sind die Klänge verhältnismäßig ruhig und erzeugen die gespannte Erwartung einer musikalischen Auflösung, die sich jedoch

From the clairvoyant bird on Yitzhak Danziger's statue *Nimrod* (1938–39) to Aviva Uri's series of drawings *Requiem to a Bird* (1977) and even, with some variation, the fleeting image of the bird in the works of Michal Naaman and Raffi Lavi from the nineteen-eighties and nineties, the bird in Israeli art had been laden with portent—no longer a biblical bearer of post-apocalyptic peace but rather a prophetic animal harboring no prophecy, traversing genres and time. This is not, of course, an isolated motif in Israeli art, for we can think of a broader trajectory that would include Max Ernst, Salvador Dalí, Robert Rauschenberg, and Louise Bourgeois, or, in music, the work of Robert Schumann, Maurice Ravel, and Olivier Messiaen.[6] Hes Yassour's bird emits a sense of terrible sadness; being caged and projected as a ghostly apparition, it is already not itself and becomes a phantasmagorical allegory for any broken promise or narcissistic consolation that art could offer but must never become.

The encounter between the "one" and the mirrored many is an essential element of all of the works in *Temp-Est*. Hes Yassour recreated the bat's nocturnal route from footage she obtained from the Weizmann Institute of Science, which she uses in *Space and its Double – Observations* in an attempt to build a life-size stereoscope, a tilted, duplicated postcard, which mirrors each other and is comprised of identical elements with slight differences. The viewer moves through darkened spaces, where he meets images that he has seen before, elevating the image into an emblem of a promise without promise met at the deadened video corridors borne of dissimilitude and threatening erasures. This is where the phantasmagoria turns in on itself and uncovers its epistemic conceit. There is no double because the very essence of the phantasmagoric questions the very possibility of an origin, be it space or its double. Jacques Derrida's reading of Antonin Artaud's *Theater and its Double* pointed to the narcissistic conceit of mirrors, doublings, and duplications.[7] For the game of overfiguration determines an instance of forgetfulness of origin, for it splits what it doubles, making any space therefore non-originary, echoed, devoid of materiality. Repetition always engages erasure and devaluation. One time, therefore, is an enigma that has no meaning, no presence, no legibility.

Penny Hes Yassour's installations play with vision, with what one sees and what disappears from view. Vision per se is tampered with, as spectators are required to assume a different order of seeing, defined by a bat-like disorientation and blindness—spatial and temporal. One is asked, so to speak, to see with his ears. Seeing does not lend itself to protocols of remembrance, let alone memory, for Hes Yassour tries to demonstrate what cannot be demonstrable. She shows us that we don't see, that memory is not opposite but is akin to an essential stupor, and that memory seldom has to do with what is seen. In its entirety, the work hones in on acts of forgetfulness, which arguably covers the same ground but is not identical to memory. Staying close to the atonalities of oblivion, Hes Yassour sketches the figural border that both art and modernity

nicht einstellt. Das Aufeinanderprallen von akustischer Stille und visueller Übersättigung animiert uns dazu, länger zu verweilen und die Diskrepanz des Kunstobjekts zu bestaunen, durch die die Identität dauerhaft unbestimmt bleibt; damit entsteht so etwas wie ein alternativer Blick, vielleicht auf überbestimmte Weise.

Auf der rechten Seite der Installation, eingeschlossen in einer Vitrine aus Holz und Glas, befindet sich das holografische Bild einer einsamen, allein gelassenen Kreatur, deren Morphologie uneindeutig bleibt; es scheint sich um eine Kreuzung zwischen einer Fledermaus und einem weißen Vogel zu handeln. Der Fledermaus-Vogel geht auf Benjamins „Engel der Geschichte“[5] zurück; beim Betrachten der sich auftürmenden Trümmer historischer Ruinen, die er mit „Fortschritt“ gleichgesetzt hatte, spreizt er anscheinend die Flügel und schaut hinüber zur anderen Seite der allseits bedrohlichen Installation, hält sich jedoch abseits davon. An dieser Stelle mag die Randfigur ohne Weiteres den Kernpunkt (im Sinne von Roland Barthes' *punctum*) des Werks bilden, genau das Zentrum, in dem es ruht oder eher einstürzt. Denn was die Kreatur sieht, ist eine unermessliche Zahl von Doppelgängern: Penny Hes Yassour hat den dämmrigen Sperrholzhimmel mit dem bewegten Bild eines Vogelschwarms ausgefüllt, der ziellos seine Kreise zieht und auf diese Weise mit unheilvoller Hitchcock-Symbolik aufgeladen ist. In der israelischen Kunst dienen Vögel häufig als Vorboten, vom hellsichtigen Vogel auf Itzhak Danzigers Statue *Nimrod* (1938/39) über Aviva Uris Zeichenserie *Requiem to a Bird* (1977) bis hin zu den leicht abgewandelten flüchtigen Vogeldarstellungen in Michal Naamans und Raffi Lavis Arbeiten aus den 1980er- und 90er-Jahren. Der Vogel ist kein biblisches Symbol für postapokalyptischen Frieden mehr, sondern eher ein prophetisches Tier ohne Prophezeiungen, das Gattungen und Zeiten durchquert. Natürlich beschränkt sich dieses Motiv nicht allein auf die israelische Kunst; auch bei Max Ernst, Salvador Dalí, Robert Rauschenberg, Louise Bourgeois oder in den musikalischen Werken Robert Schumanns, Maurice Ravels und Olivier Messiaens lässt es sich finden.[6] Hes Yassours Vogel strahlt eine schreckliche Traurigkeit aus. Eingesperrt und als geisterhafte Erscheinung projiziert, ist er schon nicht mehr er selbst, sondern wird zu einer phantasmagorischen Allegorie für alle gebrochenen Versprechen oder narzisstischen Tröstungen, die Kunst anbieten könnte, zu denen sie jedoch niemals werden darf.

Die Begegnung zwischen dem „Einen“ und den gespiegelten Vielen ist essenzieller Bestandteil aller Arbeiten in dieser Ausstellung. In *Space and its Double – Observations* vollzieht Penny Hes Yassour die nächtliche Flugroute der Fledermaus anhand von Bildmaterial des Weizmann Institute of Science nach. Es ist der Versuch, ein lebensgroßes Stereoskop zu errichten, mit zwei schräg angeordneten, spiegelbildlichen Postkarten, die die gleichen Elemente zeigen, sich jedoch geringfügig voneinander unterscheiden. Der Betrachter bewegt sich durch abgedunkelte Gänge, in denen er auf Bilder trifft, die er bereits zuvor gesehen hat; das Bild wird zum Symbol für ein hoffnungsloses Versprechen, dem man in den

designate in the realm of the specter, broaching spaces of death and venturing in the verbiages of radical non-meaning.

When Galia Bar Or first introduced me to Penny Hes Yassour, she told me, "Penny is not just an artist. Penny is a scientist." Hes Yassour had just returned from the Asian Art Biennale in Taiwan, where she had spun her chemical polymers into the hanging "double surface formations" of *I'm Writing You Tomorrow* (2011). I recall this visit to her studio at the outskirts of Kibbutz Ein Harod, where, indeed like a scientist, it seemed that she was working in pure isolation. Evoking this scene now, I think it would be more accurate to describe Hes Yassour's experimentations as pertinent to alchemy rather than science, which traditionally required this hermit-like environment and underground sensibilities. As an alchemist, one of her primary acts seems to be her uncanny ability to imbue the non-figural inanimate with soul or spirit, technologically pitched. But even here, she has never been a traditionalist, for her underground activity is conducted above ground, in plain sight, and despite its exposure manages to avoid the world of external phenomena.

Friedrich Nietzsche hierarchized the relation between art and science in *The Gay Science*, stating that everyone should study art because art was a preparation for the science of the future. The works presented in Recklinghausen seem to have taken in this Nietzschean insight, though not without a grain of doubt and marked irony (like a good Nietzschean), figured in a Kunstkammer-like display of historicity that draws our attention to the interplay between the object, the projection, and the shadow. And yet despite their materialities, the work assumes an ethereal quality, interpolating the spectator in an arhythmical dynamic that invites and at the same time expels a stable mode of reading precisely because of the panoply of scientific elements refusing their own signification. In the absence of any stable or set logic of signification, where any act of memory essentially bleeds into oblivion, abandoned or doubled and divided, what are we left with? Something nonetheless remains, without, however, becoming presence, radically sheltered in absence, as absence, as phantasmagoria that engages essential solitude, like that of Hes Yassour the alchemist. We are left wondering after shadows, forever in the dark, like a bat.

1 Walter Benjamin, *The Arcades Project,* Cambridge, MA: Harvard University Press, 1999, p. 14.

2 Benjamin 1999 (see note 1), p. 26.

3 In the *Critique of Judgment*, Immanuel Kant distinguishes between two types of the sublime: the dynamic and the mathematical. The mathematical sublime addresses a feeling of magnitude beyond all comparison, of the absolutely incalculable, which can therefore both violence and terror. See Immanuel Kant, *Kritik der Urteilskraft*, §25, Suhrkamp: Frankfurt, 1974, p. 169.

gedämpften Videokorridoren begegnet, entstanden aus Unähnlichkeit und bedrohlichen Auslöschungen. Hier zeigt die Phantasmagorie ihr wahres Gesicht und offenbart ihre epistemologische Selbstgefälligkeit. Es gibt kein Ebenbild, denn die Phantasmagorie stellt im Kern die bloße Möglichkeit eines Ursprungs infrage, sei es für den Raum oder für sein Duplikat. Jacques Derridas Interpretation von Antonin Artauds *Das Theater und sein Double* verweist auf die narzisstische Selbstgefälligkeit von Spiegeln, Verdopplungen und Wiederholungen.[7] Das Spiel mit der Überfiguration sorgt für ein Vergessen des Ursprungs, denn es spaltet auf, was es verdoppelt, und macht somit jeden Raum zu etwas Nichtursprünglichem, zu einem Widerhall ohne Stofflichkeit. Wiederholung führt immer zu Auslöschung und Abwertung. „Ein Mal" wird dadurch zu einem Rätsel ohne Bedeutung, ohne Präsenz, ohne Lesbarkeit.

Penny Hes Yassours Installationen spielen mit dem Blick: mit dem, was man sieht, und mit dem, was aus dem Blickfeld verschwindet. Sie machen sich am Blick selbst zu schaffen, denn sie verlangen vom Publikum eine andere Reihenfolge des Sehens, bestimmt von fledermausartiger Desorientierung und Blindheit – räumlich wie zeitlich. Man wird sozusagen aufgefordert, mit den Ohren zu sehen. Sehen taugt nicht für Gedächtnisprotokolle, geschweige denn für Erinnerungen. Hes Yassour versucht, das darzustellen, was nicht darstellbar sein kann. Sie zeigt uns, dass wir nicht sehen, dass Erinnerung nicht das Gegenteil von essenzieller Reglosigkeit ist, sondern damit einhergeht, und dass sie selten etwas mit dem zu tun hat, was man sieht. In seiner Gesamtheit fokussiert sich ihr Werk auf Handlungen des Vergessens, was zwar möglicherweise den gleichen Spielregeln folgt, jedoch nicht deckungsgleich mit Erinnerung ist. Hes Yassour bleibt nah bei den Atonalitäten des Vergessens und skizziert die figurale Grenze, die Kunst und Modernität im Reich des Geisterhaften gleichermaßen aufweisen, indem sie Räume des Todes eröffnen und sich in die Geschwätzigkeiten radikaler Nichtbedeutung vorwagen.

Als Galia Bar Or mich mit Penny Hes Yassour bekannt machte, sagte sie zu mir: „Penny ist nicht nur Künstlerin, sie ist Wissenschaftlerin." Hes Yassour war gerade von der Asian Art Biennial in Taiwan zurückgekehrt, wo sie ihre chemischen Polymere in die hängenden Doppelflächenformationen von *I'm Writing You Tomorrow* (2011) eingesponnen hatte. Ich erinnere mich an den Besuch in Hes Yassours Atelier am Rande des Kibbuz Ein Harod, wo sie tatsächlich wie eine Wissenschaftlerin in völliger Abgeschiedenheit zu arbeiten schien. Aus heutiger Sicht würde ich Hes Yassours Experimente wohl eher alchemistisch als wissenschaftlich nennen, denn eine derartige Vorgehensweise erfordert traditionell ein Einsiedlerdasein und untergründige Sensibilität. Als Alchemistin scheint es zu Hes Yassours grundlegenden Fähigkeiten zu gehören, dem nicht figuralen Unbelebten durch technische Hilfsmittel Seele oder Geist zu verleihen. Aber auch hierbei verfährt Hes Yassour nie traditionell, denn sie führt ihre Untergrundaktivitäten vor aller Augen durch, und es gelingt ihr, trotz der öffentlichen Zurschaustellung die Welt der Erscheinungen zu meiden.

4 Following his distinction in *Beyond the Pleasure Principle* (1918) between the death drive and eros, Freud later describes the death drive as mute: "The death instincts are by their very nature mute, and the clamour of life proceeds for the most part from Eros." (translation modified). The muteness of the death-drive is essential, as its encroachments bears no sonic cues, which makes its effect, according to both Freud and the post-Freudians, more devastating and self-destructive. See Sigmund Freud, *The Ego and the Id*, The Standard Edition of the Complete Psychological Works, Vol. 19, Vintage: London, 2001, p. 46.

5 My reference here is to the famous "Angel of History," a figure utilized by Benjamin, inspired by Paul Klee's *Angelus Novus* (1920), in order to describe the catastrophic effect of the conceit of historical progress, which for Benjamin can only be given in and as ruins. This is part of a broader philosophy of historical materialism developed by Benjamin on the brink of his suicide in 1940 and which was supposed to be incorporated into the unfinished *Arcades Project.* Walter Benjamin, "Theses on the Philosophy of History," *Illuminations*, London: Pimlico, 1998, p. 249.

6 The list here is endless, however I am thinking here of Robert Schumann's *Vogel als Prophet*, from the *Waldszenen* op. 82, Maurice Ravel's *Oiseaux tristes* from the *Miroirs* and Olivier Messiaen's monumental *Catalogue d'oiseaux*.

7 Jacques Derrida, "The Theater of Cruelty and the Closure of Representation," *Writing and Difference*, Chicago: University of Chicago Press, 1978, p. 312.

Friedrich Nietzsche hierarchisierte das Verhältnis zwischen Kunst und Wissenschaft in *Die fröhliche Wissenschaft* und tat kund, dass sich jeder mit Kunst befassen sollte, weil Kunst eine Vorbereitung auf die Wissenschaft der Zukunft sei. Die in Recklinghausen gezeigten Arbeiten scheinen diese Erkenntnis Nietzsches erfasst zu haben, wenn auch nicht ganz ohne Zweifel und deutliche Ironie (wie es sich für gute Nietzscheaner gehört). Sie präsentieren sich in einem kunstkammerartigen, geschichtsträchtigen Ambiente, das unsere Aufmerksamkeit auf das Zusammenspiel zwischen dem Gegenstand, der Projektion und dem Schatten lenkt. Aber trotz ihrer Stofflichkeit nehmen die Werke eine ätherische Qualität an und ziehen den Betrachter in eine arrhythmische Dynamik hinein, die einen stabilen Deutungsmodus gleichzeitig fordert und ausschließt, weil die sich wissenschaftlich gebenden Elemente dieser bunten Palette ihre eigene Signifikation verweigern. Und was bleibt uns noch ohne jegliche stabile oder vorgegebene Bedeutungslogik, wenn jeder Akt des Erinnerns im Grunde in die Vergessenheit ausfärbt, aufgegeben oder dupliziert und geteilt wird? Etwas bleibt trotzdem übrig, ohne jedoch gegenwärtig zu werden, streng abgeschirmt in Abwesenheit, als Abwesenheit, als Phantasmagorie, die eine essenzielle Einsamkeit erzeugt wie die von Penny Hes Yassour, der Alchemistin. Wir bleiben zurück und staunen über Schatten, für immer im Dunklen wie eine Fledermaus.

1 Benjamin, Walter: *Das Passagen-Werk,* in: ders.: *Gesammelte Schriften,* Bd. 5, hrsg. von Rolf Tiedemann, 1. Aufl. [Nachdruck], Frankfurt am Main 2006, S. 1256.

2 Vgl. ders.: *The Arcades Project,* Cambridge 1999, S. 26.

3 In der *Kritik der Urteilskraft* unterscheidet Kant zwischen dem Dynamisch- und dem Mathematisch-Erhabenen. Das Mathematisch-Erhabene wirkt durch seine unermessliche Größe, es erzeugt ein Gefühl der absoluten Unberechenbarkeit, das folglich sowohl Gewalt als auch Schrecken hervorrufen kann. Siehe Kant, Immanuel: *Kritik der Urteilskraft,* § 25, Frankfurt am Main 1974, S. 169.

4 Nach seiner Unterscheidung zwischen Todestrieb und Eros in *Jenseits des Lustprinzips* (1918) merkt Freud später an, „daß die Todestriebe im wesentlichen stumm sind und der Lärm des Lebens meist vom Eros ausgeht." Die Stummheit des Todestriebs ist essenziell, da sein Vordringen lautlos erfolgt, was seine Wirkung laut Freud und den Postfreudianern noch verheerender und selbstzerstörerischer macht. Siehe Freud, Sigmund: *Psychologie des Unbewußten,* 6. Aufl., Frankfurt am Main 1975 [= Studienausgabe, Bd. 3].

5 Ich beziehe mich hier auf den berühmten „Engel der Geschichte", der von Paul Klees *Angelus Novus* (1920) inspiriert wurde. Benjamin verwendet die Figur, um die katastrophale Wirkung der Wahnidee vom geschichtlichen Fortschritt aufzuzeigen, die er für ganz und gar desaströs hält. Dies ist Teil einer umfassenderen Philosophie des historischen Materialismus, die von Benjamin kurz vor seinem Selbstmord 1940 entwickelt wurde und sich ursprünglich in das unvollendete *Passagen-Werk* einfügen sollte. Siehe Benjamin, Walter: „Über den Begriff der Geschichte", in: ders.: *Gesammelte Schriften,* Bd. I, Frankfurt am Main 1980, S. 697.

6 Die Liste ist endlos, allerdings denke ich hauptsächlich an Schumanns *Vogel als Prophet* aus den *Waldszenen,* op. 82, an Ravels *Oiseaux tristes* aus *Miroirs* und an Messiaens monumentalen *Catalogue d'oiseaux.*

7 Vgl. Derrida, Jacques: „Das Theater der Grausamkeit und die Geschlossenheit der Repräsentation", in: ders.: *Die Schrift und die Differenz,* übers. von Rodolphe Gasché, 8. Aufl., Frankfurt am Main 2000.

ERODED LANDSCAPES

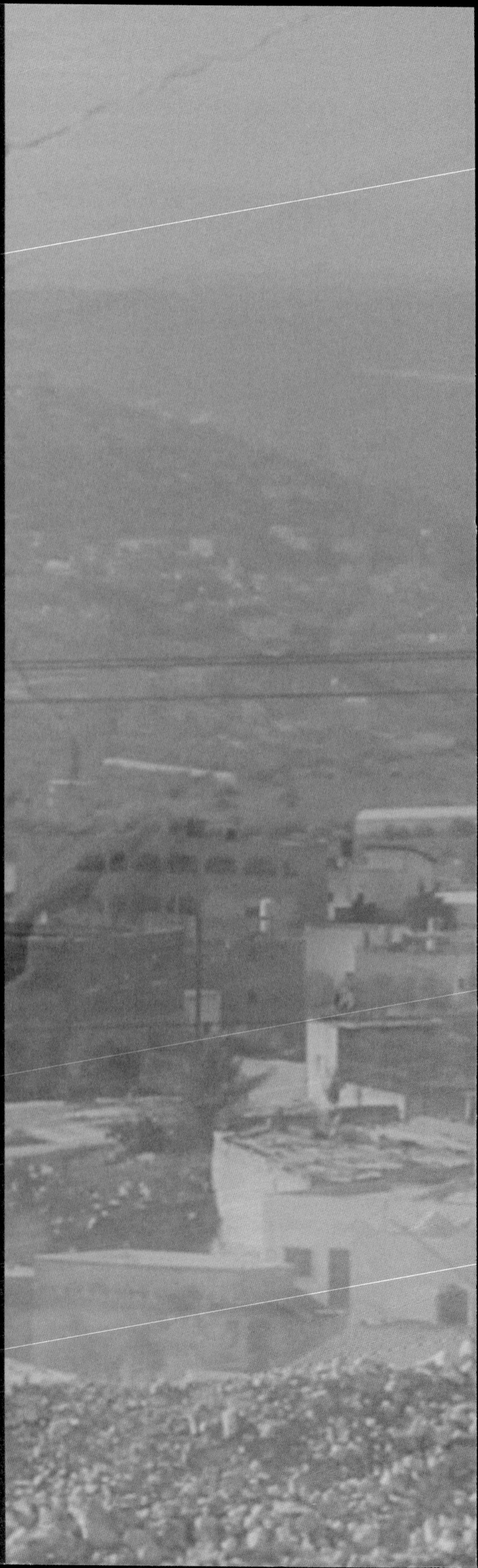

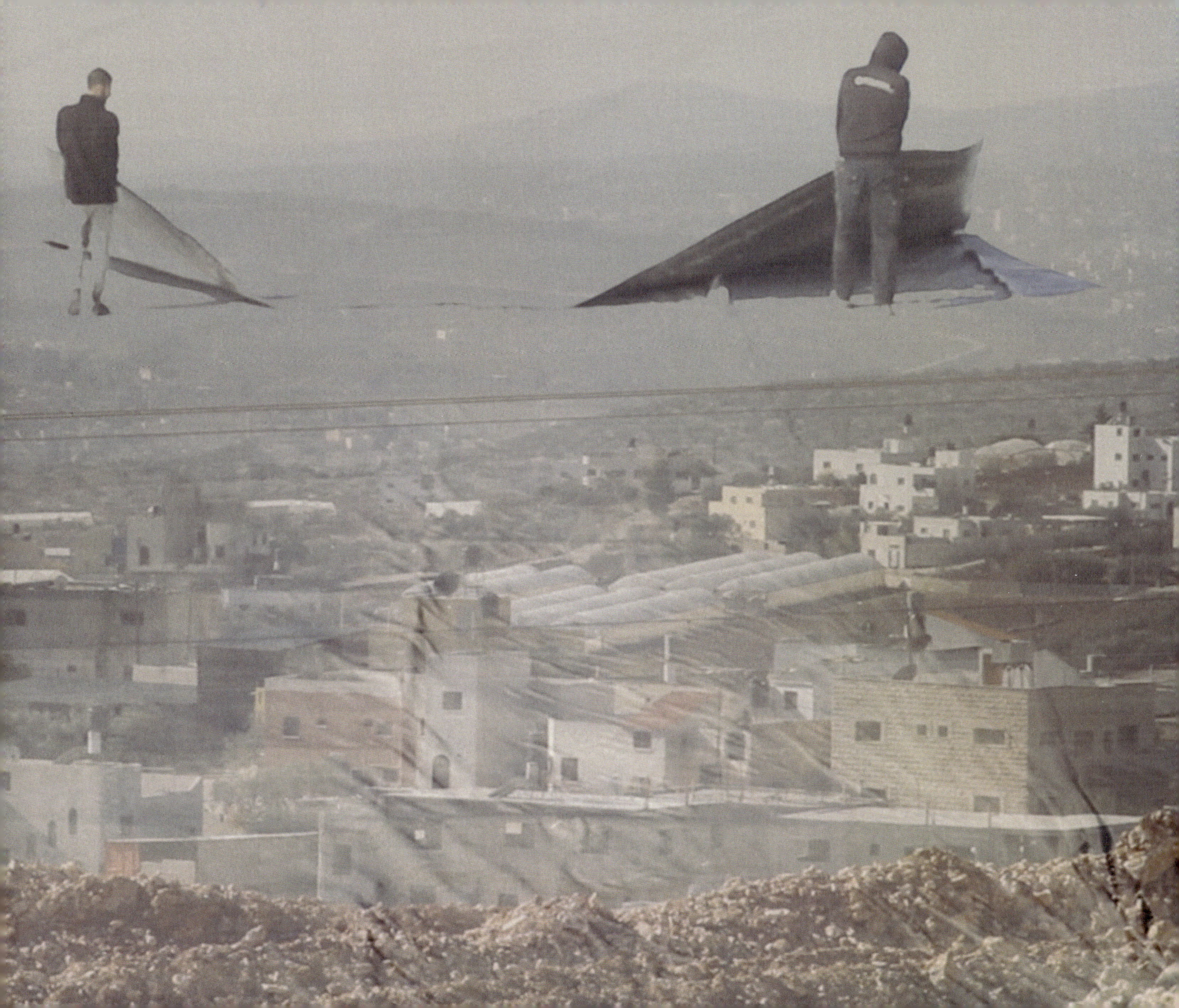

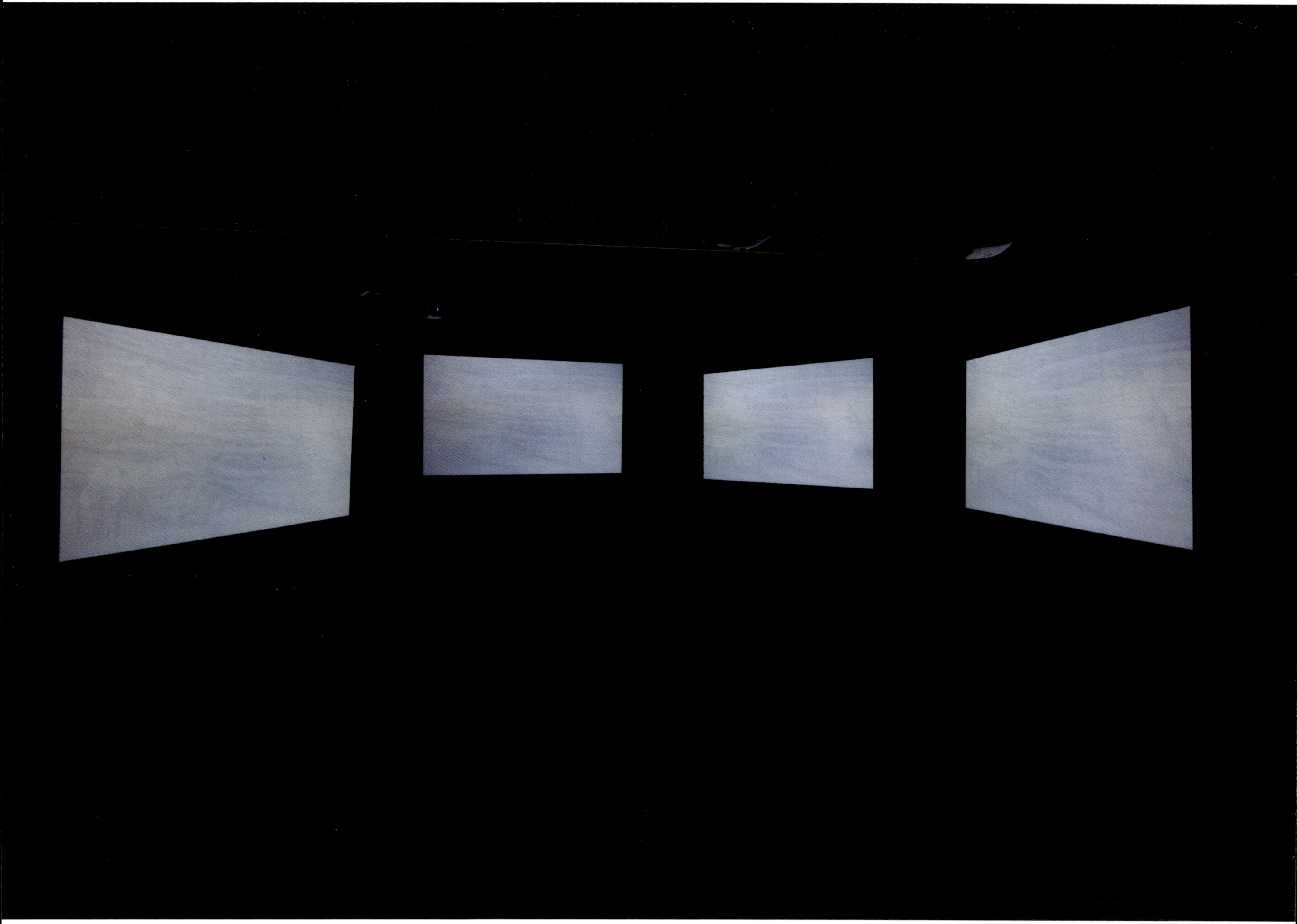

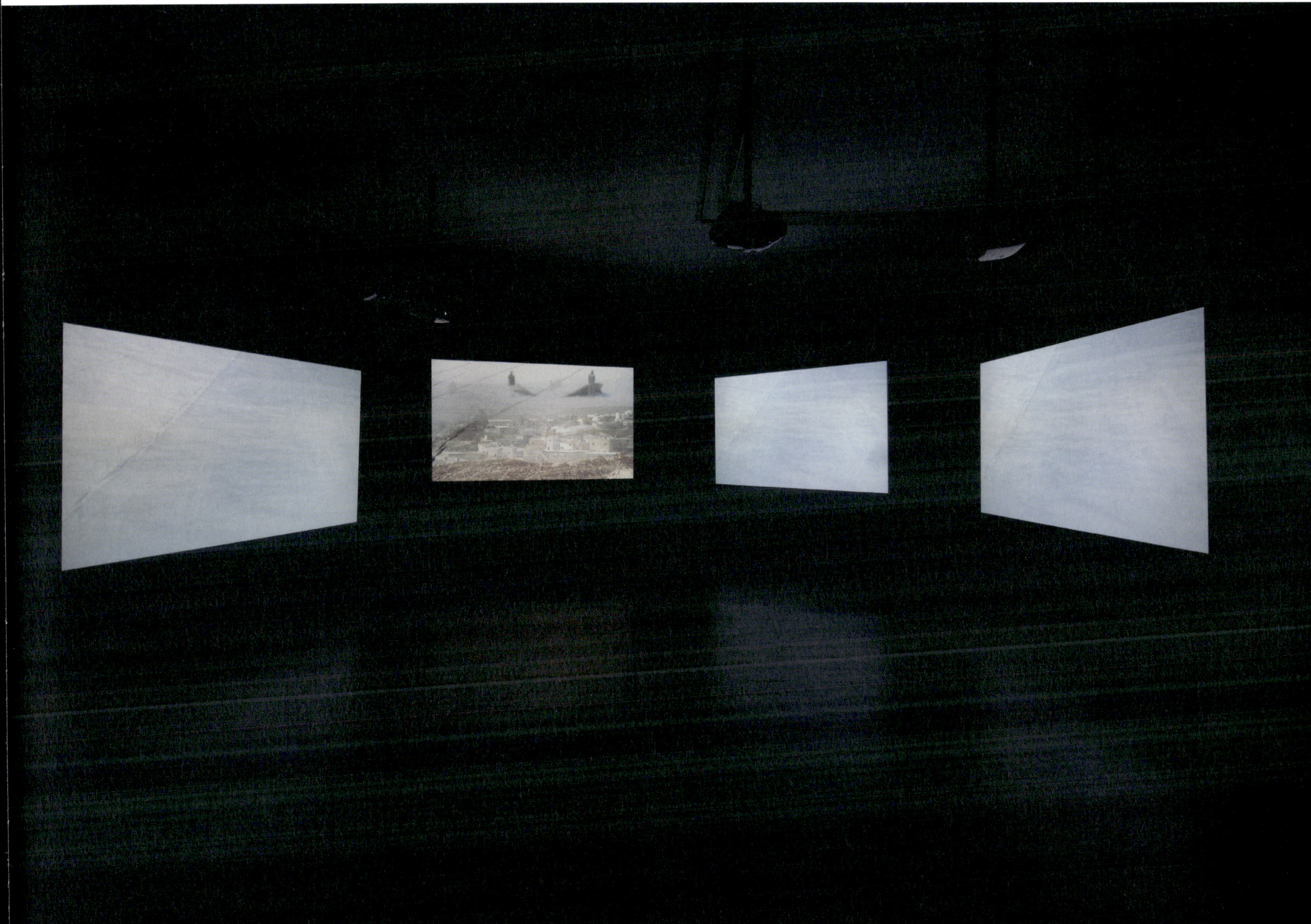

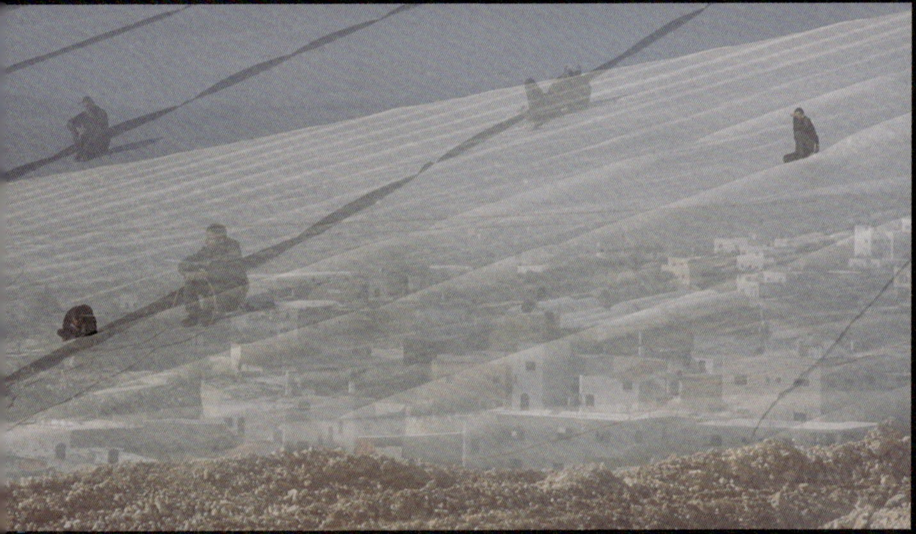
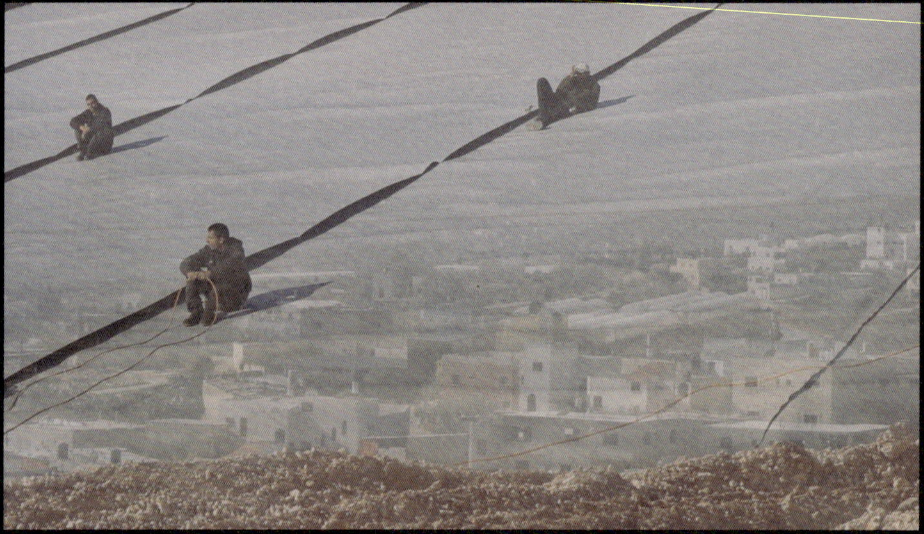
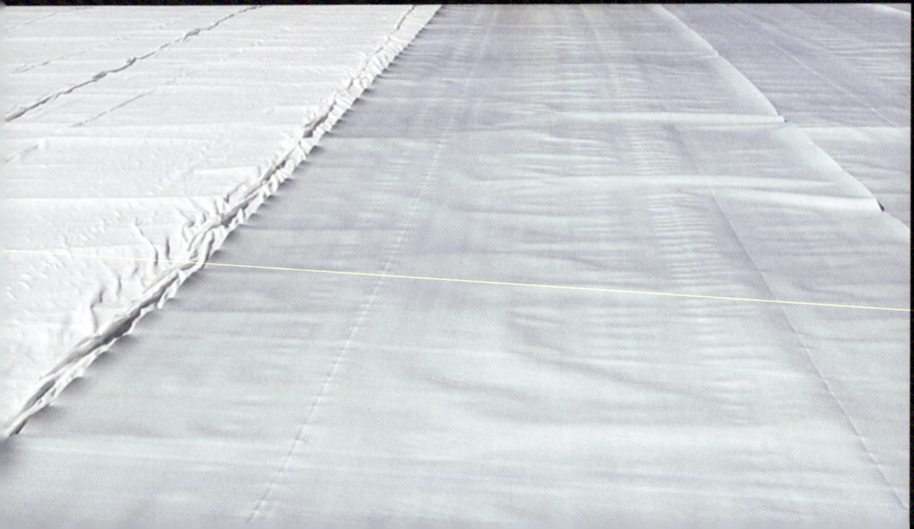
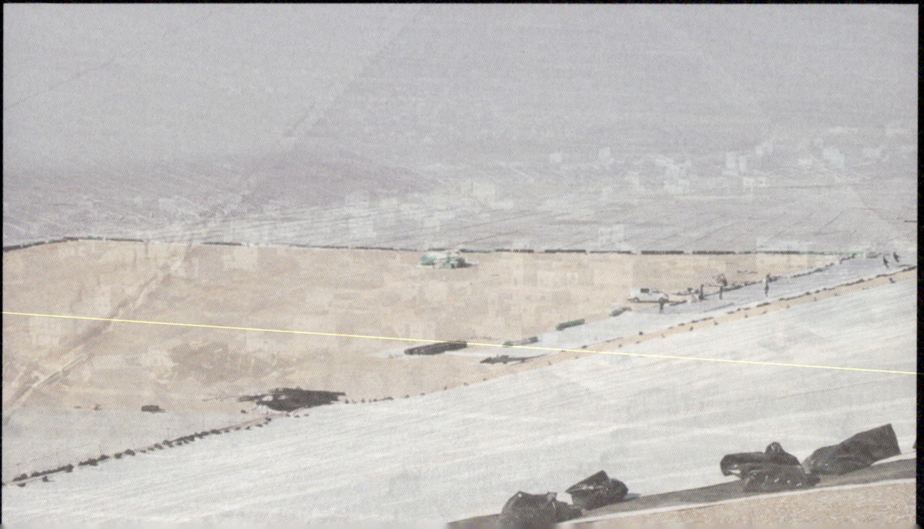

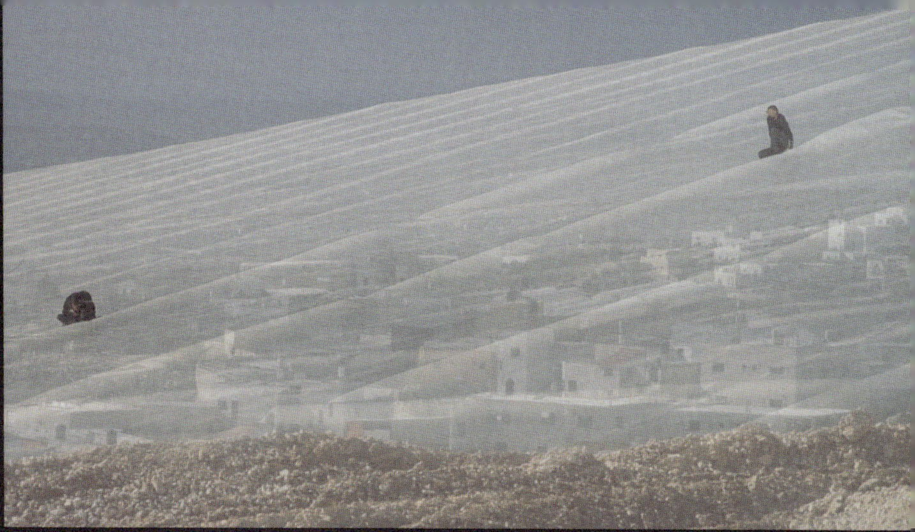
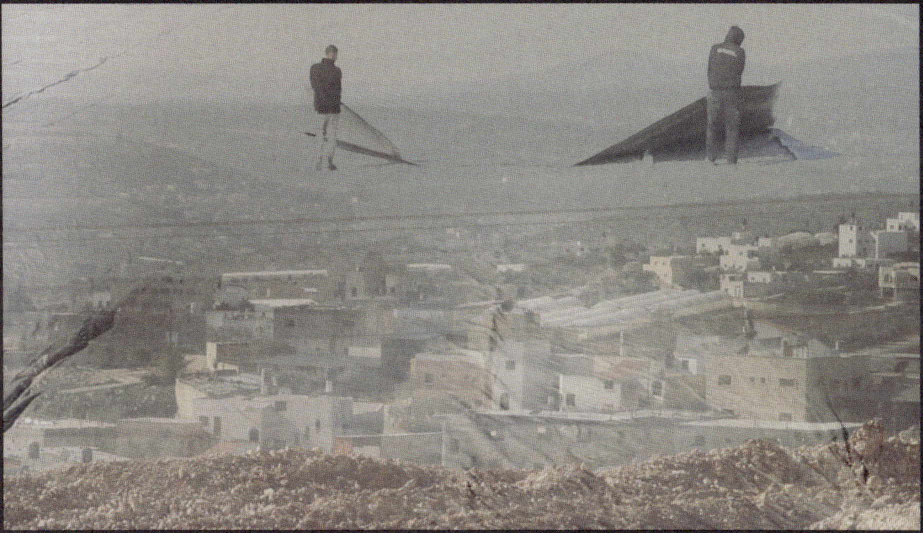
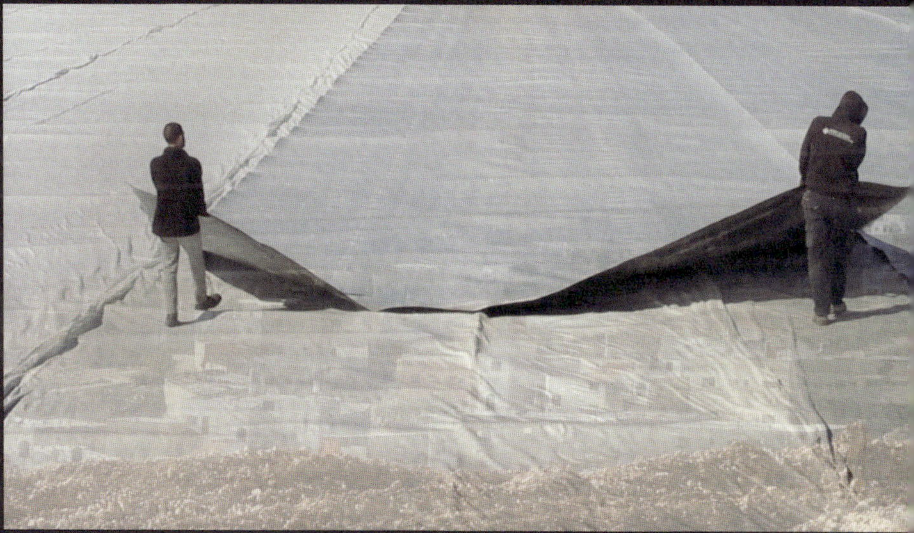
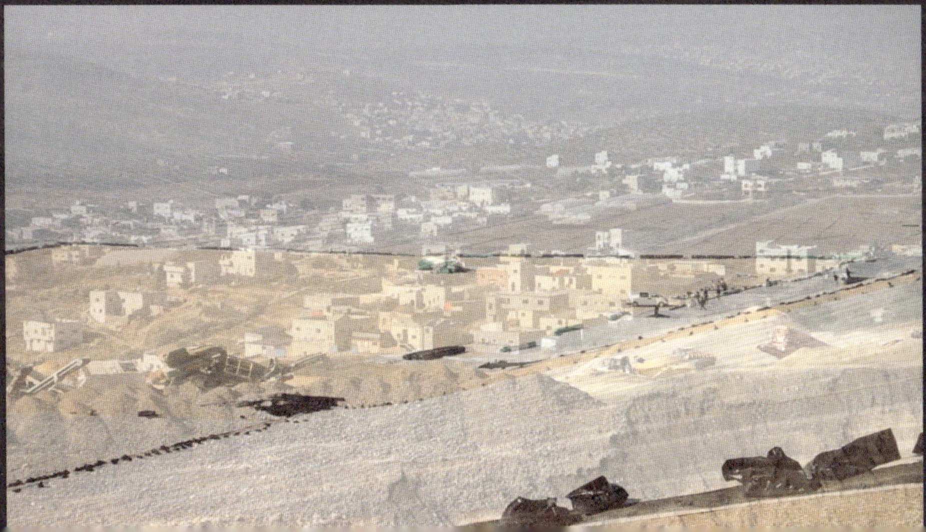
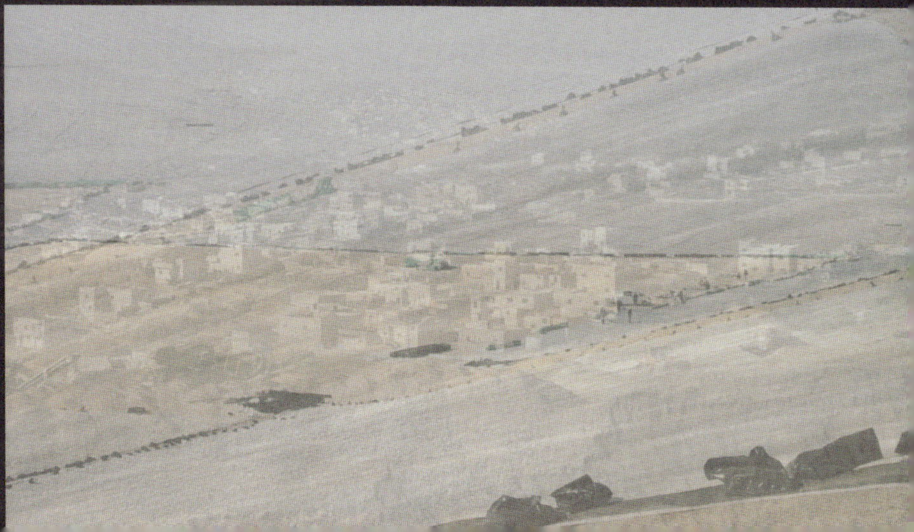

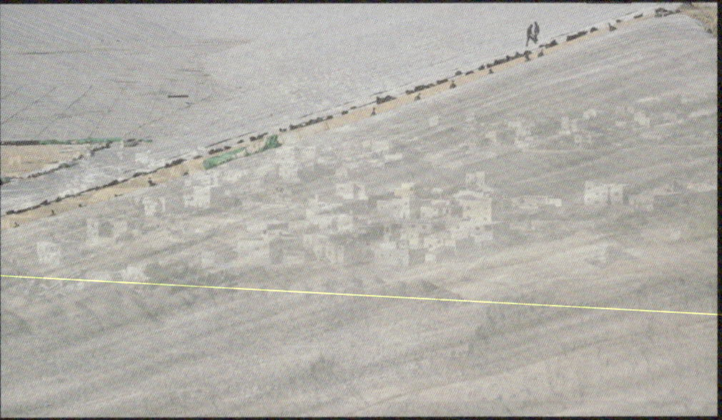
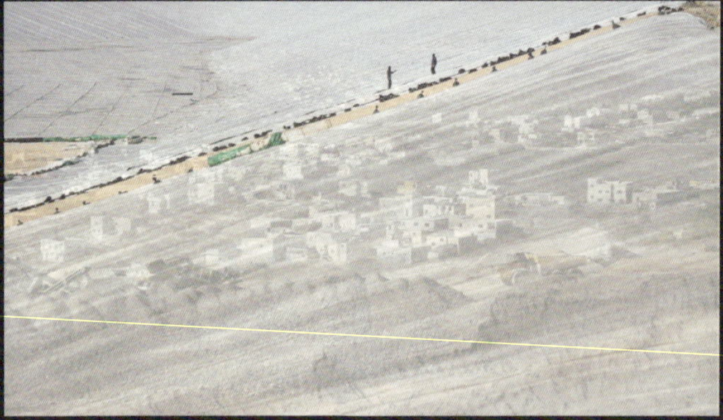
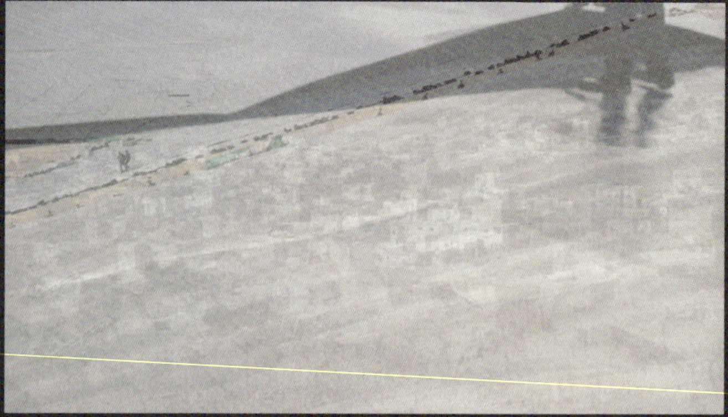
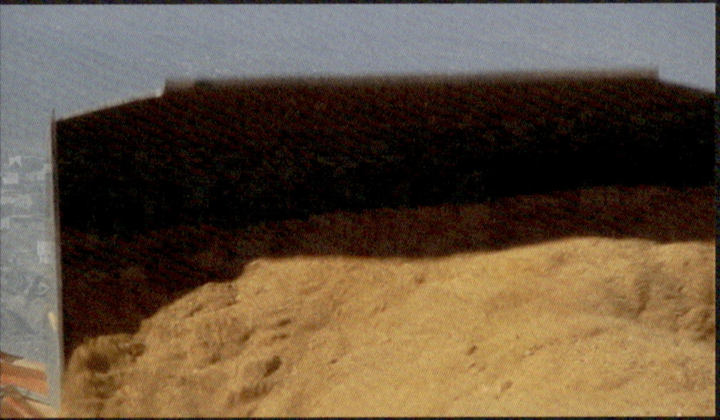
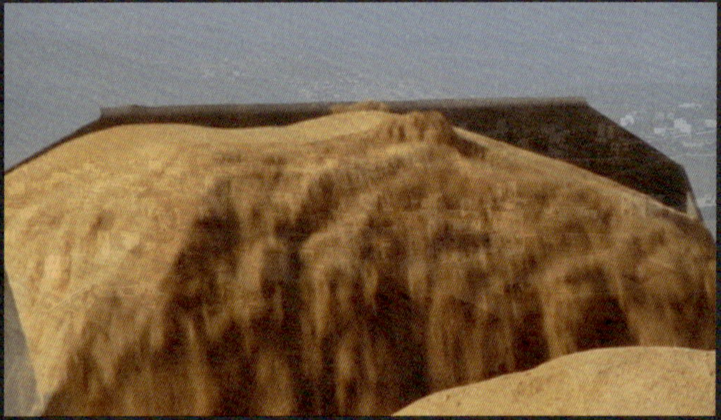
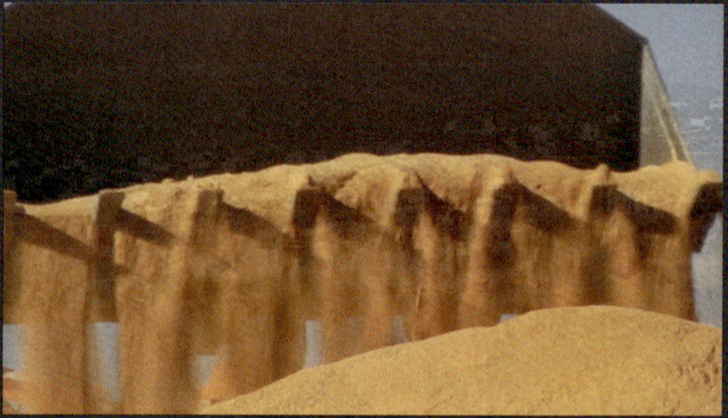
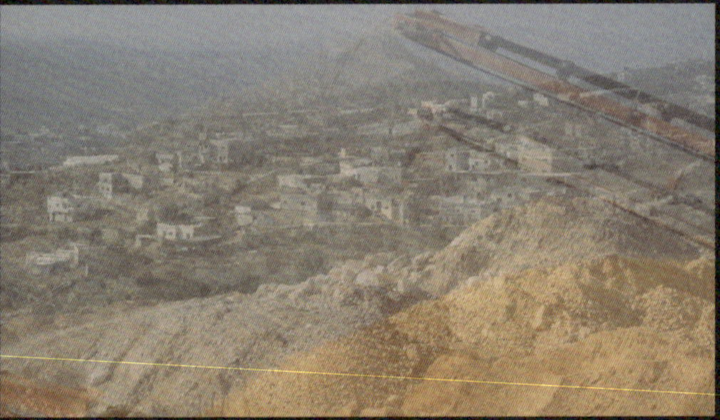
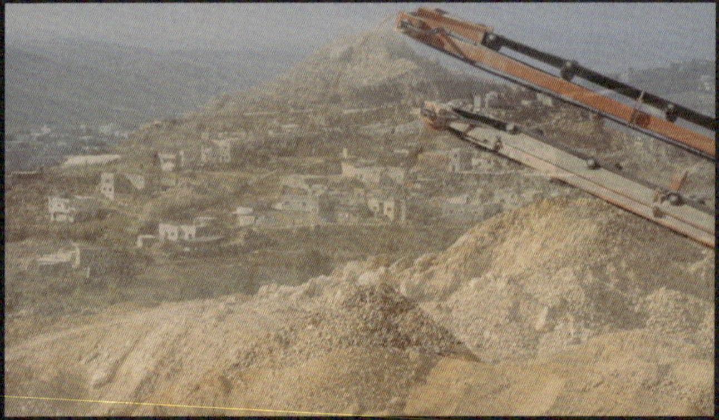
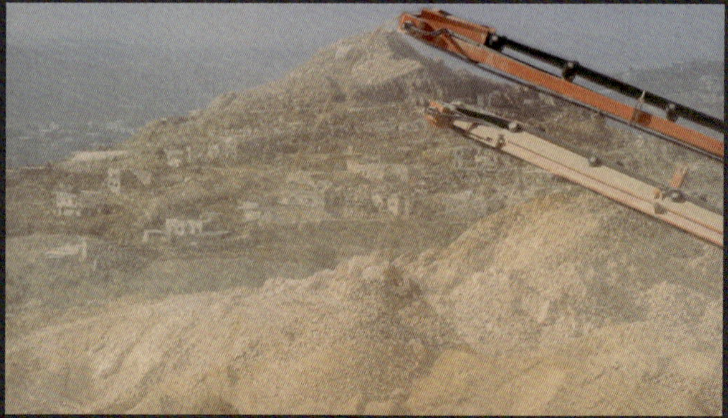

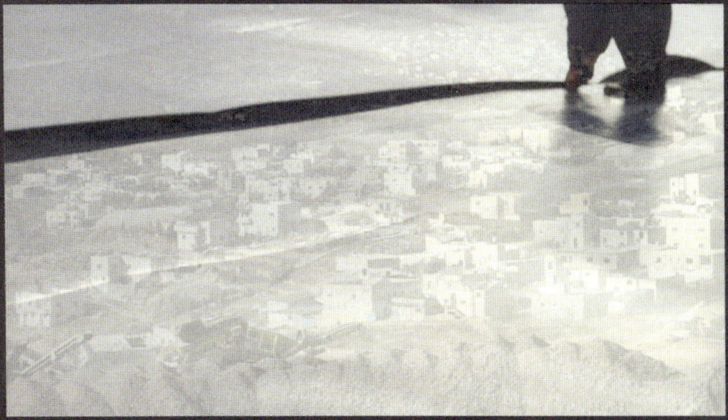
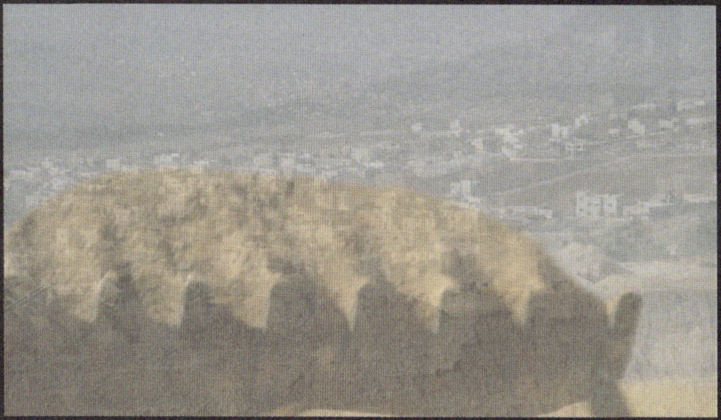
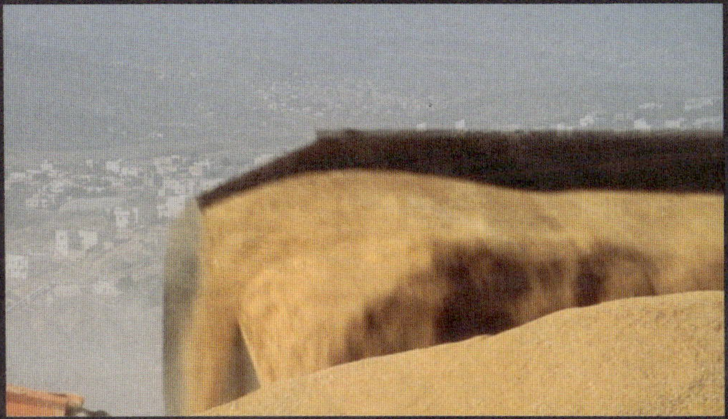
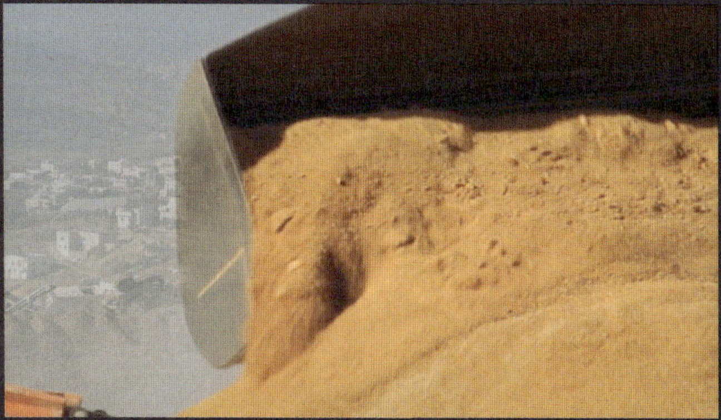
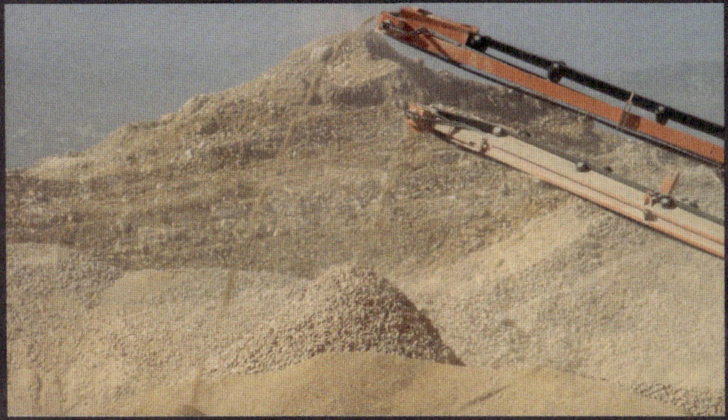

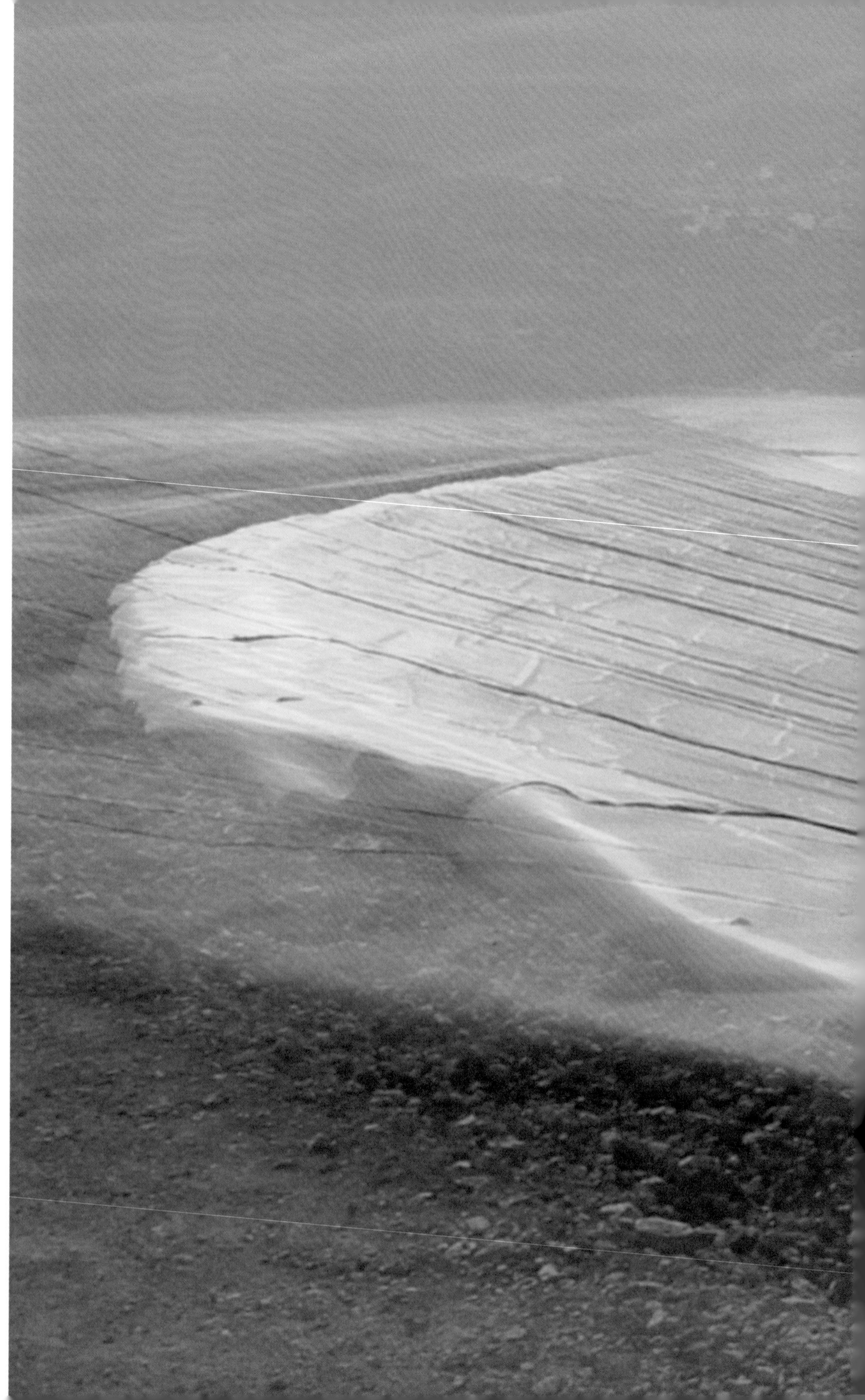

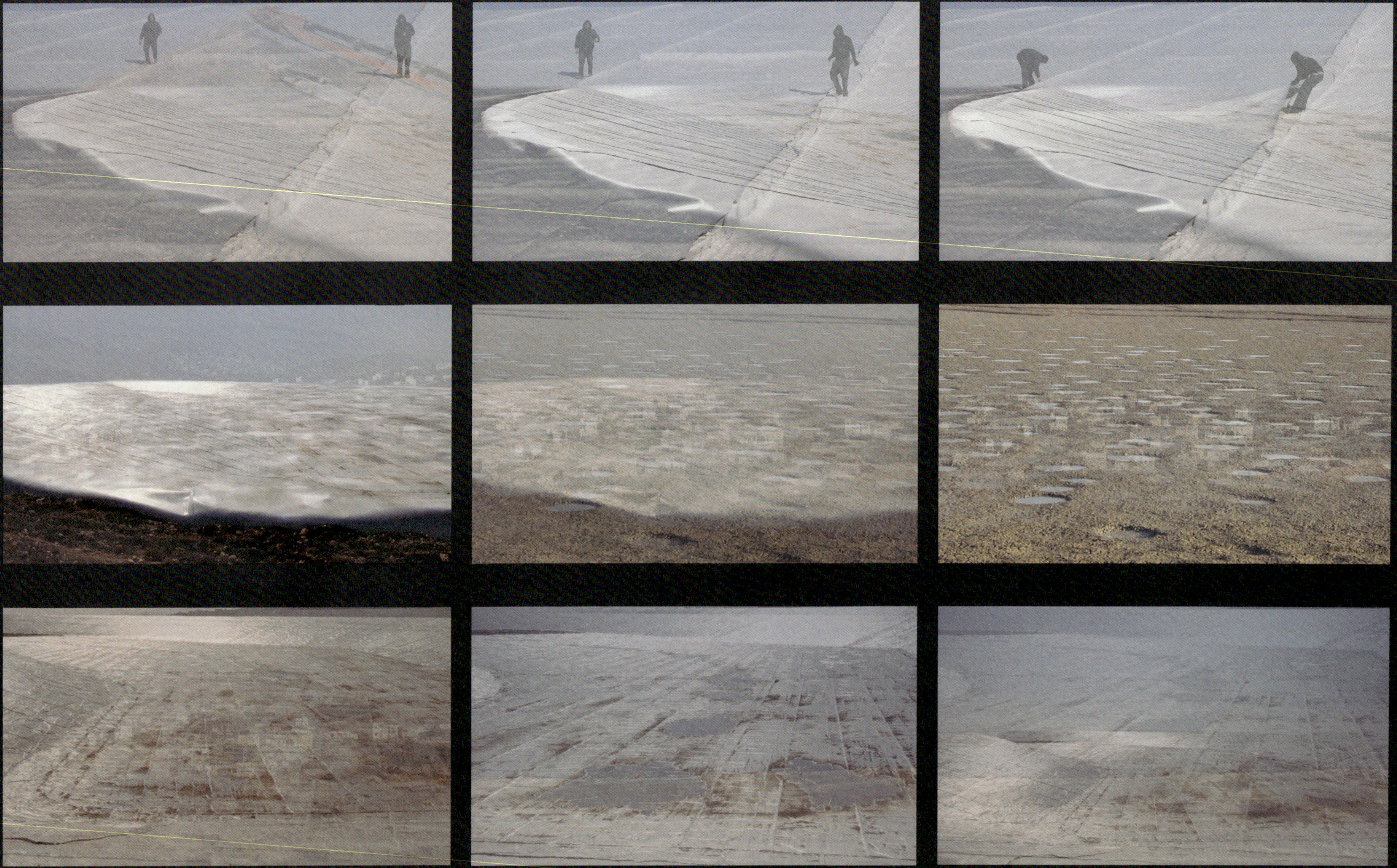

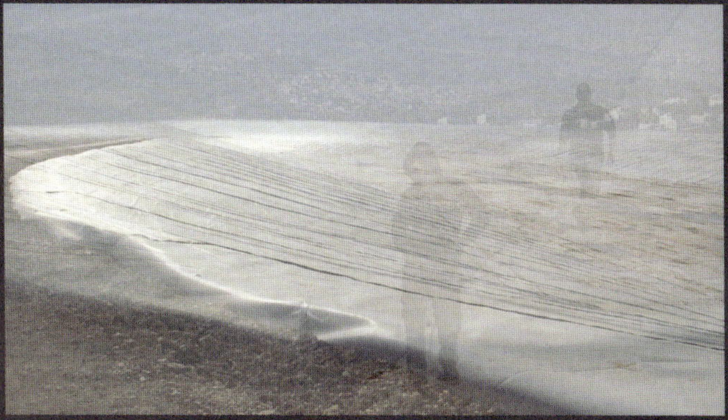
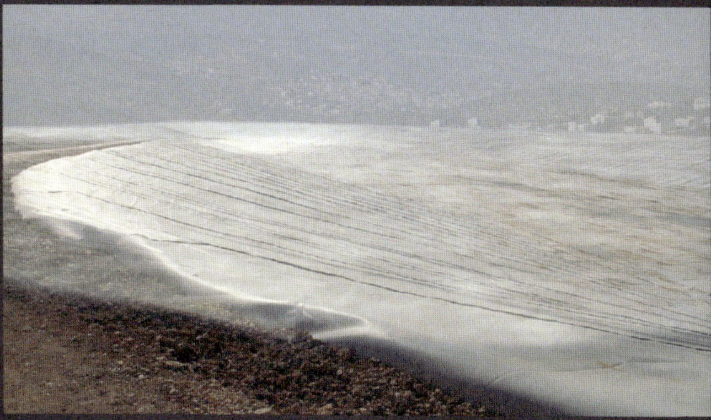
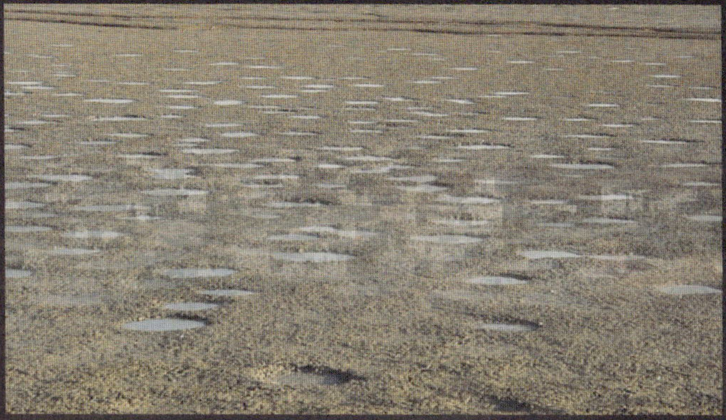
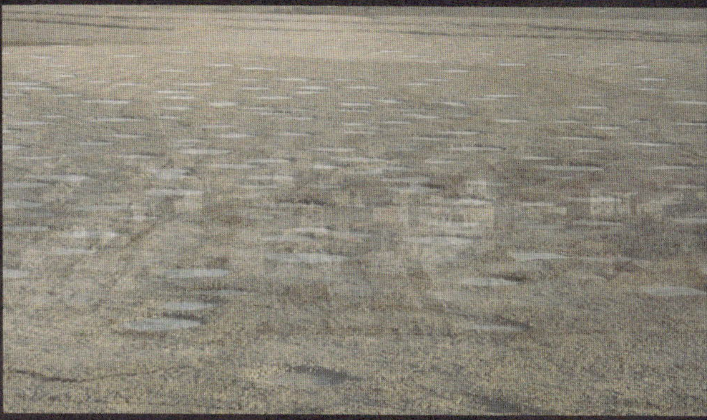

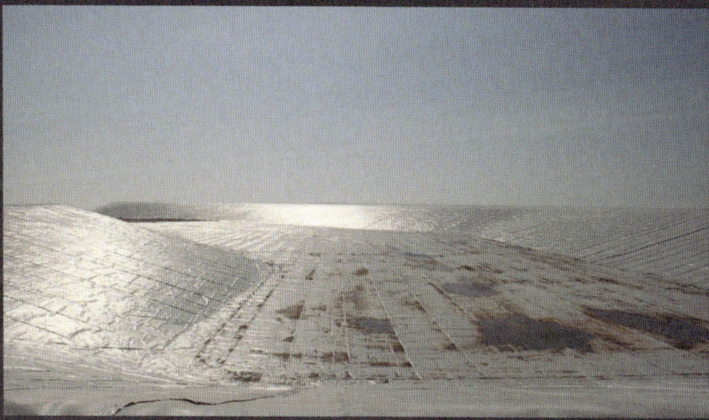

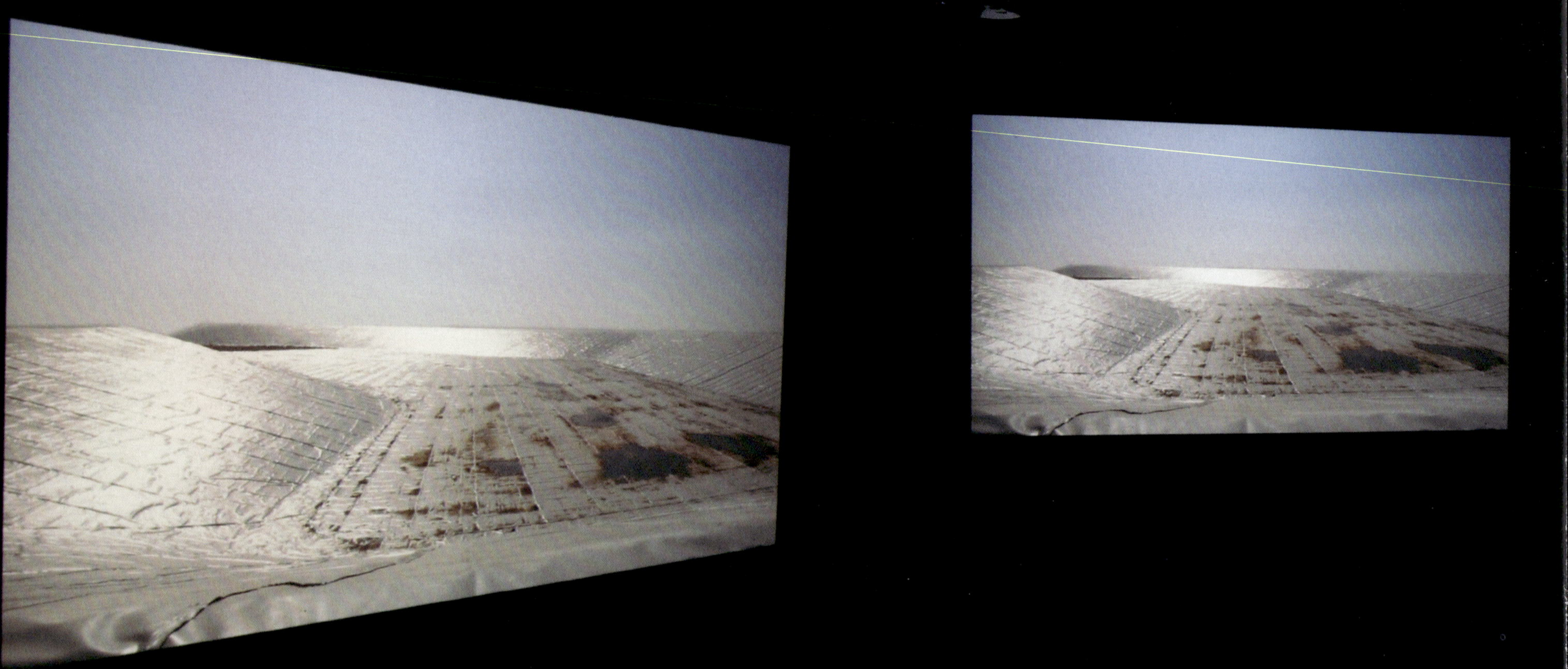

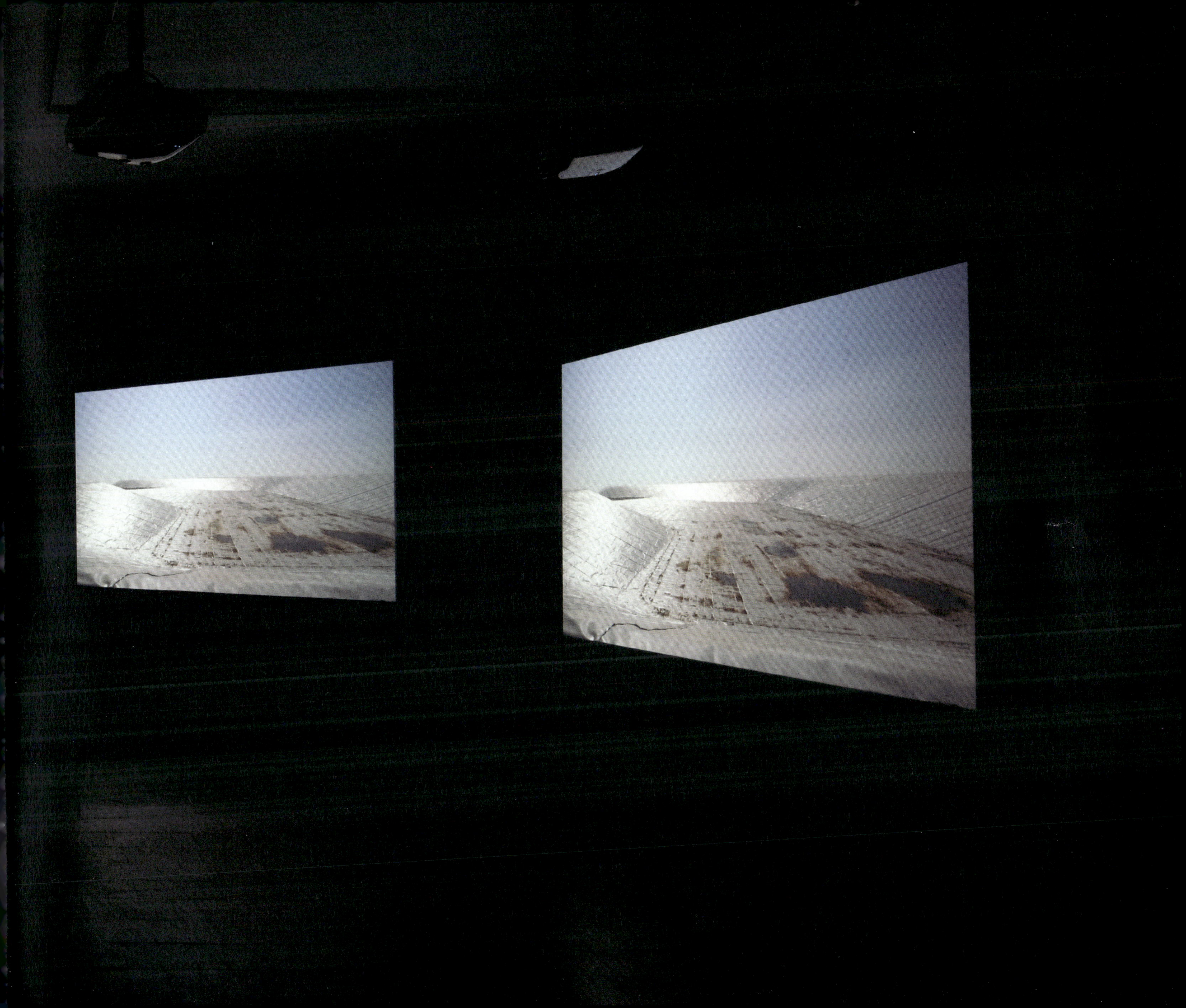

BIOGRAPHY

Penny Hes Yassour lives and works at Kibbutz Ein Harod (Ihud), Israel.

Has taught at the Architecture Department and the Interdisciplinary Department at Bezalel Academy of Arts and Design, Jerusalem, since 2000

Studied Fine Art and Geography at Haifa University and Art History at Tel Aviv University

TEACHING POSTS AND RESIDENTIAL SCHOLARSHIPS

2017 Guest professor, workshop mentor at Bard College Berlin, A Liberal Arts University

2015–17 Artist in residence, Alexander Silberman Institute of Life Sciences, Hebrew University, Jerusalem

2016 Guest professor, studio mentor at HafenCity University Hamburg

2014 Artist in residence at the Department of Music, Braun Music Center, Stanford University, California

ACCOLADES

2009 Prize for Excellence in the Arts, given for the first time, Israel National Lottery Council for the Arts

2003 Prize of the Minister of Culture, Israel

2000 Award of the Adolph & Esther Gottlieb Foundation, New York

1999 Arnold Bode Award of the documenta City of Kassel for the contribution to documenta X, Kassel, 1997

1994 Prize of the Visual Arts Department, Ministry of Science and the Arts, Israel

SOLO EXHIBITIONS AND PROJECTS (SELECTION)

2019 *Temp-Est*, art exhibition of the Ruhrfestspiele Recklinghausen, Kunsthalle Recklinghausen (D)

2016/17 *Mapping of Countries Yet to Come*, Wilfrid Israel Museum, Kibbutz Hazorea (IL)

2014 *I Am Writing You Tomorrow*, USC Pacific Asia Museum, Pasadena (USA)

2011 *I Am Writing You Tomorrow*, Asian Art Biennial, National Taiwan Museum of Fine Arts, Taichung (RC)

2009 Stage set for William Shakespeare's *The Tempest*, directed by Jarg Pataki, Theater Freiburg, Freiburg im Breisgau (D)

2009 *Phantom Landscapes*, Stux Gallery, New York (USA)

Phantom Landscapes, Galerie Eric Dupont, Paris (F)

2008/09 *Kibbutz*, with Patrick Feigenbaum, Kunstmuseum Bochum (D)

2007 dsArt Galerie, Frankfurt am Main (D)

Deep Skin, Herzliya Museum of Contemporary Art, Herzliya (IL)

2005/06 *... And I Was Filled with Shame and Fear*, installation for the exhibition *Light Art from Artificial Light*, ZKM | Zentrum für Kunst und Medientechnologie, Karlsruhe (D)

2005 *GreenBlueprint (Lament)*, BauHausFischer, Wuppertal (D)

2004 *After Images: Kunst als soziales Gedächtnis*, Neues Museum Weserburg, Bremen (D)

Spatial Drafts, Gordon Gallery, Tel Aviv-Jaffa (IL)

2003 *UnseenScene: 10. Brief*, Kunsthaus Hamburg, Hamburg (D)

UnseenScene: 10. Brief, Oldenburger Kunstverein, Oldenburg (D)

UnseenScene (9th Letter), Haifa Museum of Art, Haifa (IL)

2001 *The Irrationality of Rationality Itself*, installation for the exhibition *Israeli Art Today*, The Museum of Modern Art, Saitama (J)

2000/01 *Echolalia*, Kasseler Kunstverein, Fridericianum, Kassel (D)

1999 *Space Is Never Less Than Doubled or Daddy Dear, Come to the Luna-Park*, Mishkan Museum of Art, Ein Harod (IL)

1998 *La ville d' à côté / Unmentionable Neighborhood*, MAC, Galeries contemporaines des Musées de Marsille (F)

1997/98 *Mental Maps – Involuntary Memory*, presented in conjunction with *German Art from Beckmann to Richter: Images from a Divided Country*, Martin-Gropius-Bau, Berlin (D)

1997 *Mental Maps – Involuntary Memory*, documenta X, Kassel (D)

1993 *Mental Maps – Production Halls*, Mishkan Museum of Art, Ein Harod (IL)

BIOGRAFIE

Penny Hes Yassour lebt und arbeitet im Kibbuz Ein Harod (Ihud) in Israel.

Unterrichtet seit dem Jahr 2000 an den Fachbereichen für Architektur und interdisziplinäre Studien der Bezalel Academy of Arts and Design in Jerusalem

Studierte Kunstwissenschaft und Geografie an der Universität Haifa sowie Kunstgeschichte an der Universität Tel Aviv

LEHRAUFTRÄGE UND AUFENTHALTSSTIPENDIEN

2017 Gastprofessorin und Workshopmentorin am Bard College Berlin, A Liberal Arts University

2015–2017 Artist in Residence am Alexander Silberman Institute of Life Sciences der Hebräischen Universität in Jerusalem

2016 Gastprofessorin und Studiomentorin an der HafenCity Universität Hamburg – Universität für Baukunst und Metropolenentwicklung

2014 Artist in Residence am Braun Music Center innerhalb des Fachbereichs Musik der Universität Stanford in Kalifornien

AUSZEICHNUNGEN

2009 Prize for Excellence in the Arts des Israel National Lottery Council for the Arts (erstmals verliehen)

2003 Auszeichnung des israelischen Kulturministeriums

2000 Preis der Adolph & Esther Gottlieb Foundation in New York

1999 Arnold-Bode-Preis der documenta-Stadt Kassel für den Beitrag zur documenta X in Kassel 1997

1994 Preis der Abteilung für bildende Kunst des israelischen Ministeriums für Wissenschaft und Kunst

EINZELAUSSTELLUNGEN UND PROJEKTE (AUSWAHL)

2019 *Temp-Est,* Kunstausstellung der Ruhrfestspiele Recklinghausen, Kunsthalle Recklinghausen (D)

2016/17 *Mapping of Countries Yet to Come,* Wilfrid Israel Museum, Kibbuz Hazorea (IL)

2014 *I Am Writing You Tomorrow,* USC Pacific Asia Museum, Pasadena (USA)

2011 *I Am Writing You Tomorrow,* Asian Art Biennial, National Taiwan Museum of Fine Arts, Taichung (RC)

2009 Bühnenbild für William Shakespeares *The Tempest (Der Sturm)* unter der Regie von Jarg Pataki, Theater Freiburg, Freiburg im Breisgau (D)

Phantom Landscapes, Stux Gallery, New York (USA)

Phantom Landscapes, Galerie Eric Dupont, Paris (F)

2008/09 *Kibbuz,* mit Patrick Faigenbaum, Kunstmuseum Bochum (D)

2007 dsART Galerie, Frankfurt am Main (D)

Deep Skin, Herzliya Museum of Contemporary Art, Herzliya (IL)

2005/06 *… And I Was Filled with Shame and Fear,* Installation für die Ausstellung *Lichtkunst aus Kunstlicht,* ZKM | Zentrum für Kunst und Medientechnologie Karlsruhe (D)

2005 *GreenBlueprint (Lament),* BauHausFischer, Wuppertal (D)

2004 *After Images. Kunst als soziales Gedächtnis,* Neues Museum Weserburg, Bremen (D)

Spatial Drafts, Gordon Gallery, Tel Aviv-Jaffa (IL)

2003 *UnseenScene. 10. Brief,* Kunsthaus Hamburg (D)

UnseenScene. 10. Brief, Oldenburger Kunstverein, Oldenburg (D)

UnseenScene (9th Letter), Haifa Museum of Art, Haifa (IL)

2001 *The Irrationality of Rationality Itself,* Installation für die Ausstellung *Israeli Art Today,* Museum of Modern Art, Saitama (J)

2000/01 *Echolalia,* Kasseler Kunstverein, Fridericianum, Kassel (D)

1999 *Space Is Never Less Than Doubled or Daddy Dear, Come to the Luna-Park,* Mishkan Museum of Art, Ein Harod (IL)

1998 *La ville d'à côté / Unmentionable Neighborhood,* MAC, Galeries contemporaines des Musées de Marseille (F)

1997/98 *Mental Maps – Involuntary Memory,* vorgestellt in *Deutschlandbilder – Kunst aus einem geteilten Land,* Martin-Gropius-Bau, Berlin (D)

1997 *Mental Maps – Involuntary Memory,* documenta X, Kassel (D)

1993 *Mental Maps – Production Halls,* Mishkan Museum of Art, Ein Harod (IL)

IMPRESSUM | IMPRINT

AUSSTELLUNG | EXHIBITION

Penny Hes Yassour
Temp-Est

Kunstausstellung der
Ruhrfestspiele Recklinghausen 2019

Kunsthalle Recklinghausen
5.5.–14.7.2019

Konzeption | Concept
Penny Hes Yassour
Nerya Shohat
Hans-Jürgen Schwalm
Kerstin Weber

Medientechnik | Media Technology
Paul Trinker

Aufbau und Technik | Technical Staff
Klaus-Dieter Riedel
Marc Braunstein
Gebhard Meier
James Larsen
Peter Schloss

Verwaltung | Administration
Monika Cienkusz
Zemira Ruznic-Pupovic
Marcus John

Ruhrfestspiele Recklinghausen

Festspielleiter und Geschäftsführer | Artistic Director and Executive Director
Olaf Kröck

Geschäftsführerin und Verwaltungsdirektorin | Executive Director and Administrative Director
Genia Nölle

KATALOG | CATALOGUE

Herausgeber | Editors
Hans-Jürgen Schwalm
Kerstin Weber

Konzeption und Gestaltung | Concept and Design
Penny Hes Yassour
Hans-Jürgen Schwalm
Kerstin Weber

Layout | Graphic Design
Ute Lübbeke

Fotografie | Photographs
Alistair Overbruck

Übersetzung | Translation
Eva-Raphaela Jaksch · Tradukas GBR
Uri Bruck

Lektorat | Copyediting
Julia Frohnhoff
Wendy Brouwer

Schrift | Typeface
Transat und Adobe Caslon

Papier | Paper
LuxoArt Samt

Die Deutsche Nationalbibliothek verzeichnet diese Publikation in der Deutsche Nationalbibliografie; detaillierte bibliografische Daten sind im Internet über http://dnb.dnb.de abrufbar.

The Deutsche Nationalbibliothek lists this publication in the Deutsche Nationalbibliografie; detailed bibliographic data are available on the Internet at http://dnb.dnb.de.

Gesamtherstellung und Vertrieb | Printed and published by
Edition Cantz
Dieselstraße 50
73734 Esslingen
www.edition-cantz.de

Druck | Print
Dr. Cantz'sche Druckerei Medien GmbH, Esslingen

Printed in Germany

ISBN Verlag 978-3-947563-48-7
ISBN Museum 978-3-939753-79-7

Frontispiz | Frontispiece
Atelier der Künstlerin, 2019
The artist's studio, 2019

Space and its Double – Observations
2017–2019
Photographer – Nerya Shohat
Editors – Penny Hes Yassour, Nerya Shohat

Resonance Towers – between Memory and Oblivion 2017–2019
Photographer – Nerya Shohat
Editors – Penny Hes Yassour, Nerya Shohat
Sound composer – Jonathan Berger

a·ban·don·ment 2017–2019
Photographer – Nerya Shohat
Editors – Penny Hes Yassour, Nerya Shohat

Eroded Landscapes 2018–2019
Photographer – Nerya Shohat
Editors – Penny Hes Yassour, Nerya Shohat, Erez Miller
Sound composer – Jonathan Berger